D0661127

Secrets
of the
BEST
Choice

The Riverboat Adventures

1. *Escape Into the Night*
2. *Race for Freedom*
3. *Midnight Rescue*
4. *The Swindler's Treasure*
5. *Mysterious Signal*
6. *The Fiddler's Secret*

Adventures of the Northwoods

1. *The Disappearing Stranger*
2. *The Hidden Message*
3. *The Creeping Shadows*
4. *The Vanishing Footprints*
5. *Trouble at Wild River*
6. *The Mysterious Hideaway*
7. *Grandpa's Stolen Treasure*
8. *The Runaway Clown*
9. *Mystery of the Missing Map*
10. *Disaster on Windy Hill*

Let's-Talk-About-It Stories for Kids

Secrets of the Best Choice
You Are Wonderfully Made!
You're Worth More Than You Think!

LET'S TALK ABOUT IT
STORIES FOR **Kids**

Secrets
of the
BEST
Choice

LOIS WALFRID
JOHNSON

BETHANY HOUSE PUBLISHERS
MINNEAPOLIS, MINNESOTA 55438

Secrets of the Best Choice
Revised Edition 1999. Copyright © 1988, 1999
Lois Walfrid Johnson

Cover by Lookout Design Group, Inc.

With the exception of "Are You a Quitter?" and "A Look in the Mirror," which are based on true incidents, the stories and characters in this book are fictitious. Any resemblance to actual persons, living or dead, is coincidental.

Unless otherwise identified, Scripture quotations are from the HOLY BIBLE, NEW INTERNATIONAL VERSION®. Copyright © 1973, 1978, 1984 by International Bible Society. Used by permission of Zondervan Publishing House. All rights reserved. The "NIV" and "New International Version" trademarks are registered in the United States Patent and Trademark Office by International Bible Society. Use of either trademark requires the permission of International Bible Society.

Scripture quotations identified NASB are taken from the NEW AMERICAN STANDARD BIBLE®, Copyright © 1960, 1962, 1963, 1968, 1971, 1972, 1973, 1975, 1977, 1995 by the Lockman Foundation. Used by permission.

Scripture quotations identified NKJV are from the New King James Version of the Bible. Copyright © 1979, 1980, 1982, by Thomas Nelson, Inc., Publishers. Used by permission. All rights reserved.

Scripture quotations identified TEV are from the Bible in Today's English Version (*Good News Bible*). Copyright © American Bible Society 1966, 1971, 1976, 1992

All rights reserved. No part of this publication may be reproduced, stored in a retrieval system, or transmitted in any form or by any means—electronic, mechanical, photocopying, recording, or otherwise—without the prior written permission of the publisher and copyright owners.

Published by Bethany House Publishers
A Ministry of Bethany Fellowship International
11400 Hampshire Avenue South, Minneapolis, Minnesota 55438
www.bethanyhouse.com

Printed in the United States of America by
Bethany Press International, Minneapolis, Minnesota 55438

Library of Congress Cataloging-in-Publication Data
Johnson, Lois Walfrid.
    Secrets of the best choice / by Lois Walfrid Johnson. — Rev. ed.
       p.   cm. — (Let's talk about it stories for kids)
    ISBN 1-55661-652-X (pbk.)
    1. Teenagers—Conduct of life. 2. Teenagers—Religious life. 3. Christian life. I. Title. II. Series: Johnson, Lois Walfrid. Let's talk about it stories for kids (Bethany House)
    BJ1661.J57   1999
    248.8'2 — dc21   99–6620
                                                                    CIP

To
Gail and Daryl,
Jeff and Cynthia,
Kevin and Lyn
because you've made great choices
and to
every kid who loves
ADVENTURES OF THE NORTHWOODS
and
THE RIVERBOAT ADVENTURES

Hang on tight to Jesus!

LOIS WALFRID JOHNSON is the bestselling author of more than twenty-five books. Her work has been translated into twelve languages and has received many awards, including the Gold Medallion, the C. S. Lewis Silver Medal, the Wisconsin State Historical Society Award, and five Silver Angels from Excellence in Media. Yet Lois believes that one of her greatest rewards is knowing that readers enjoy her books.

In all that she does, Lois seeks to live what she believes. She and her husband, Roy, are former teachers and have used the principles Lois writes about with their own children and the children they've taught. The Johnsons presently make their home in Minnesota.

Contents

To the Kids Who Read This Book

Oops! Company's coming! Your room looks like a tornado hit, and you have just twenty minutes to clean.

Well, only one thing to do. Take the dirty socks, the gym shoes, the balls, the books, the crumpled blouse or shirt, the twice-worn jeans. Shove them under the bed. Then put on a happy face. Smile. Outwardly you have a clean room.

All of us have times when we'd like to hide another kind of dirty socks. You probably know how it feels. You want to take everything you're thinking and feeling and push it under the bed. Isn't it easier to pretend you don't see whatever you don't like? To act as if it isn't there?

Yet the pressure builds up. You not only have a messy hidden place. Because you have so many feelings scrunched down inside, you're like a balloon ready to burst.

There's another way: talking about what bothers you. Getting things out in the open. Connecting with that right person who listens and lets you talk. He or she will understand how you feel and build you up rather than tear you down.

If you don't know a person like that, ask God for someone who loves you as He does—just the way you are. Maybe it will be a mom or dad, a grandparent, uncle, or aunt. It might be a neighbor, teacher, pastor, or friend.

When you find that person, start talking. Bring things out from under the bed. You'll find that something special happens. Not every problem is suddenly solved, but the right person helps you see what's happening from a different angle. Instead of feeling alone, you know there's someone who wants the best for you.

In each of the stories that follow, kids face the kind of problems you know about. These kids need to choose between right and wrong or between something good and something better. Put yourself in their shoes. Ask, "What would I do if this were happening to me or one of my friends?"

As you think and talk about the questions at the end of each story, you'll see new ways of making choices—new ways of dealing with those things that bother you. Then turn the book upside down to read the Bible verse that's given. Repeat that verse to yourself until you receive the hope and courage it gives. Pray the prayer or one of your own.

You'll catch on to something big. If you wonder whether something is right or wrong, **it helps to use the Bible in your choices.** Often there's a story or verse that fits exactly what you need to know. Other times it's important to think about the *overall* teaching of the Bible. For instance, God tells us to love one another. As you wonder about doing something, ask yourself, "Would it *help* someone (to show love)? Or would it hurt that person?"

You already may have learned to ask the question "What would Jesus do?" Take the next step. Pray, "Jesus, what do you want me to do?" Be honest with Him. Tell Him right up front, "I need your help."

Remember when you were a little kid learning to cross the street? Your mom expected you to hang on tight to her hand. Or maybe you were learning to fish. When you got a big one, Dad shouted, "Hang on tight!" You clenched that pole with all your strength. If you hadn't, the fish would have gotten away, the pole spinning through the water after him.

Or you might like amusement park rides. Think of those big swings where the seat hangs on a long chain hooked to a high center pole. When the ride starts out, you're on the ground. The faster you go, the higher you swing, and the farther out you whirl. You have to hang on tight to stay safe!

That's what it means to hang on tight to Jesus. Whatever you face, He wants to take your hand, to be there with you. In every choice you make, with every step you take, He wants to help you. He *will* if you let Him.

So are you ready? If you **hang on tight to Jesus,** you'll discover something—secrets of the best choice!

11

Are You a Quitter?

For three days Jessica had looked forward to this moment. Standing on the corral fence, she watched as her cousin Nate slipped a bridle over his pony's head.

"Reggie's a good pony," he said. "I've been riding him for three years."

Jessica glanced at two larger horses drinking water at a trough. They seemed so tall that she was glad to start out on a pony. Yet she felt sure she could handle any horse well.

"I'll give you a lift," Nate said. Jessica put one foot in his clasped hands and swung up over Reggie's bare back. "Lay your rein on the right side of his neck, and he'll turn left. Lay it on the left side, and he'll go right."

Moments later Jessica was off. As she and Reggie started down the drive, she felt excited, then sure of herself. *I knew I could handle it*, she thought.

Soon they reached a place where the road ran close to the pasture. As Jessica passed by, the other horses ran straight for the fence. Without warning, Reggie plunged away from them. As he went right, Jessica went left. With a jolt she landed in the middle of the road.

"Ouch!" she groaned. Too stunned to move, she felt shaken in every bone of her body.

"Are you okay?" called Nate, running to help.

"Stupid horse!" answered Jessica. "I won't try that again."

But Nate had a different idea. "You need to get back on."

"Are you kidding?" asked Jessica.

"You don't have to be afraid," Nate said. "He's never thrown me. He was frightened by the horses coming at him."

"But Reggie is your pony. He likes you."

"Are you a quitter?" Nate asked. "If you don't get back on now, you'll be too afraid to try again. Besides, Reggie has to know you're boss, or he'll think he can get by with throwing people."

"Well . . . maybe you're right." Slowly Jessica stood up. "The longer I think about it, the more scared I get."

Nate led Reggie to a stump. "This time I'll ride with you. You first, I'll hold him."

A moment later they were off. Soon Jessica's fear disappeared. She even started to feel excited. After a while Nate slid off.

By the end of the afternoon, Jessica felt like a seasoned rider. *What if I had missed this?* she asked herself. *What if I hadn't tried again?*

TO **TALK** ABOUT

▸ What do you especially like to do?

▸ Were you good at it the first time you tried, or did you

have to make a choice the way Jessica did?

▸ In real life Jessica became such a good rider that she won a zone championship—a six-state competition in the Hunter/Jumper class. How can that give you courage in what you're trying to learn?

▸ If you're afraid to try something, should you always try it anyway? Does God sometimes use fear or uneasiness to protect you from doing some things? Give some examples.

▸ Are there other times when God wants you to keep trying, even though it's hard? Describe some way in which you feel that you have failed. How can you get up and try again?

For God has not given us a spirit of fear, but of power and of love and of a sound mind. 2 Timothy 1:7 (NKJV)

Jesus, you know how scared I get about doing something new. Show me if I'm uneasy because you want to protect me. But if there's something you want me to learn, help me start over again and keep on trying. I need your help, Jesus, your Holy Spirit power. Thank you!

No One Will Know

Jake had agreed to baby-sit Nick and Tommy Dahlberg, but now he wished he'd stayed at home. The boys gave him trouble right from the start. They wouldn't eat the supper their mom had left for them. They didn't want to change into their pajamas. When Jake finally got them to bed, they kept asking for water.

At last the boys fell asleep, and Jake sat down to watch his favorite TV program. As it reached the most exciting point, he heard a key in the lock. The boys' parents were home. Jake would miss the end of the show!

"Have a good evening?" Mr. Dahlberg asked.

For a moment Jake wondered what to say. "Sure," he answered at last.

"Everything go okay?" asked Mrs. Dahlberg.

"Fine," Jake said. "Just fine." *Nothing I couldn't handle, even though it was awful*, he thought.

Taking the money Mr. Dahlberg held out, Jake stuffed it in his jacket pocket. *They can't pay me enough to make this evening worth it.*

Not until he reached his room at home did Jake unroll the bills. *Hmmm, maybe I'm wrong.* Tucked between two five-dollar bills was a fifty. "Wow! Mr. Dahlberg outdid himself! All that money for just one evening's work!"

Then a thought struck him. *With this and what I've saved, I'll have enough for that expensive jacket I want!*

A moment later Jake's excitement vanished. *Maybe it was a mistake. Maybe Mr. Dahlberg thought he was giving me three fives. Or two fives and a one.*

Still thinking about it, Jake crawled into bed. *Well, Mr. Dahlberg won't miss the money. They went out to eat. He'll think he lost it somewhere.*

Jake turned out the light, and the room seemed much darker than usual. A quiet little voice seemed to speak to his mind. "I should return the fifty, shouldn't I, God?"

But Jake pushed away the idea as quickly as it came. *Those kids were so awful, I earned that money! Maybe God wants to reward me for all my hard work.*

For some reason sleep wouldn't come. Jake rolled over, then back again. The dark seemed to press down on him. *What should I do? Tell Mr. Dahlberg? Or buy that jacket tomorrow?*

TO **TALK** ABOUT

▸ Do you think God was rewarding Jake for his hard work? Does God use dishonest ways to bless people with money?

▸ What do you think Jake did with the fifty-dollar bill?

▸ **When you make a choice, there will be good or**

bad consequences. Something will happen as a result of your choice. If you make a good choice, there are usually good consequences. If you make a bad choice, there are usually bad consequences. If Jake chooses to keep the fifty dollars, what kind of consequences could there be? What do you think will happen?

▸ If Jake keeps the money and no one finds out, how will he feel about himself? Explain.

▸ If Jake returns the money, what kind of consequences do you think there will be? Describe what you think will happen.

▸ In a few years, Jake might try to get a steady part-time job somewhere. How do you think Jake will feel about asking Mr. Dahlberg for a reference? Give reasons for your answer.

For you were once darkness, but now you are light in the Lord. Walk as children of light. Ephesians 5:8 (NKJV)

Jesus, it's so easy to think that no one will ever know if I keep things in the dark. But you would know. Help me to be honest in the way I live. I want to be pleasing to you.

Popcorn Plus

All week Dusti had looked forward to this slumber party. Ever since Amanda invited her, she'd thought, *How can I be so lucky? They're the "in" group at school. And they asked me!*

For a long time, Dusti had wanted to be friends with Amanda and Tish and Kim. Now was her chance!

Standing on the front step of Amanda's house, sleeping bag in one hand and overnight bag in the other, Dusti felt the first twinge of uneasiness. She remembered that her friend Erin and three other girls were also having a party that night. She had helped to plan it.

Then came Amanda's invitation, and Dusti decided she would tell Erin that she'd rather be with the other girls. That had been a bad moment.

"Oh," Erin had said. A cloud seemed to enter her clear blue eyes. Then she tried to cover up how she felt. *"Well, have a good time."*

As Dusti punched the doorbell, she tried to push the memory aside.

Amanda swung the door open wide. "C'mon in, Dusti."

Clothes and sleeping bags spread out on the floor, the girls soon gathered in a circle in the family room. *This is great!* Dusti thought as she munched chips and popcorn and listened to Tish tell a story.

Suddenly everyone laughed. *What for?* Dusti didn't understand, but she pasted a smile on her lips and pretended that she did.

When it was Kim's turn, her story was long and drawn out. This time Dusti did understand. She felt dirty all over. The hotness started inside and crept up into her neck and cheeks. Could they tell how embarrassed she was? It was hard to pretend she was laughing.

"It's your turn, Dusti." Amanda gave her a poke.

Dusti looked at the floor. "I . . . I don't know your kind of stories."

"You don't? Where have you been? In church all your life?"

Dusti swallowed around the lump in her throat. "Yes, that's right. I've been in church." Too embarrassed to meet their gaze, she looked down and began twisting the bottom of her sweat shirt.

"Hey, leave her alone," said Kim. "I go to her church, too."

"You do?" asked Amanda. "But you know more stories than any of us."

Now Kim looked embarrassed. "Well, yes." Then her face brightened as though a joke were coming. "I'm what people call a fence-sitter, I guess. One foot in the church and one in the world."

The others laughed, but Dusti felt sick inside. She jumped up, seeking escape in an upstairs bedroom. There she stayed as long as she could by combing her hair at least a hundred times. Finally she went back to the family room. As she entered the room, the conversation stopped.

Must have been talking about me, Dusti thought. A strange despair made her cold all over.

Then suddenly everyone began talking again. Around her the conversation flowed like a stream swollen by rain in spring. It seemed that no one could say anything good about her teachers.

Well, I guess teachers are fair game, Dusti told herself. *But do they have to go that far?* She reached for the popcorn, hoping to hide her uncomfortable feelings by eating.

Then the conversation shifted again. For some reason everyone kept talking about the girls Dusti usually did things with.

They're my friends, Dusti thought. *Until now I never realized how much I like them. But what should I do? Defend them? I'm afraid to.*

A moment later the meanness centered on her friend Erin. Dusti could stand it no longer. She jumped up, anger filling every part of her body. "That's not true, that's not true!" she cried out. "She's my best friend. She never did what you said!"

Amanda pulled her back down. "Hey, kid," she said. "What are you getting so excited about?"

Too miserable to answer, Dusti crawled into her sleeping bag. *How could something I thought would be so nice be so awful? This is more than I bargained for. Worst of all, I'm missing out on a party with my real friends. Will this terrible night ever end?*

TO **TALK** ABOUT

▸ Do kids in groups other than your own sometimes seem more "in," or more special, than they really are?

▸ Dusti needed God's help, and the Bible shows us someone who felt the same way. When God told King Solomon to ask for whatever he wanted, Solomon said, "Give me the wisdom I need to rule your people with justice and to know the difference between good and evil" (1 Kings 3:9, TEV). How would God's wisdom help you know what people are really like? Can you remember a time when kids you know made you uncomfortable with what they were doing? Explain.

▸ Describe some ways in which Jesus knew what people were like. For clues see John 1:45–49; Mark 2:6–8; John 2:24; John 4:28–29.

▸ When the party became too much for Dusti, she escaped upstairs. What else can you do when kids tell dirty stories?

▸ What do you think Dusti should tell her friend Erin? What qualities do you value in your best friends?

If any of you lack wisdom, you should pray to God, who will give it to you; because God gives generously and graciously to all. James 1:5 (TEV)

Forgive me, Jesus, for wanting something that seems better just because I don't have it. Give me your wisdom and understanding to know what is good, or not so good, or even wrong. Give me friends that help and support me in the way you want me to live. Thank you!

More Than a Game

Alex glanced around the field in back of his house, then swung into line opposite his three cousins and Uncle Ted. *One more touchdown and we'll have 'em,* he thought.

He checked his own line. His older brother, Matt, at right end. Sam, his cousin, in front of the pigskin. On the far left, his little sister, Kristin.

Inwardly Alex groaned. What could Kristin do? But with Dad gone, even now on Thanksgiving Day, they were short one person. Would Kristin remember their secret play?

Hands on knees, Alex crouched. *I wonder what Dad's doing today,* he asked himself as he often did.

With the question came the familiar tightening of his stomach. *I don't think I can stand to eat—especially not the big bird. Was it my fault that Dad moved out? Sometimes he got awfully mad at me.*

Every muscle ready to move, Alex waited for the ball to go into play. Yet he couldn't push thoughts of his dad aside. *It's the first Thanksgiving he hasn't played with us.*

Sam snapped the ball into Alex's hands. Alex faded back,

looking for Matt. His brother was racing down the right side, but he was covered.

Alex pivoted. There was Kristin on the left, down by the goal line and completely open. He drew back his arm, and the football made a long spiral through the air.

"C'mon, Kristin, catch it! Just once!" he wanted to shout.

Arms in a circle, she stood there with eyes squeezed shut. The ball dropped through her arms like a basketball and hit her stomach. As she hugged the ball, it stayed.

Kristin opened her eyes, surprise written across her face.

"Go for it!" Alex shouted. "Over the goal line!"

Turning, Kristin took five steps and fell into the end zone.

"Yaaaaaay!" the shout went up. Even the other team called, "Lookin' good, Kristin!"

Alex and Matt slapped her on the back. "Way to go!"

But Dad isn't here to see it, thought Alex. *And he won't be carving the turkey, either.*

His mother's call interrupted them. "Your dad's on the phone," she said. "You first, Alex. We'll wait to eat."

Fifteen minutes later Alex dropped into his dining room chair and bowed his head. For the first time, he had asked his dad, "Was it my fault you and Mom got divorced?"

"Oh no, Alex!" his dad said. "The problem was between your mother and me. I love you as much as I always have."

As Uncle Ted led the prayer, Alex had more to think about than food. *Thank you, God,* he prayed without speaking aloud. *Thank you that my dad still loves me.*

TO TALK ABOUT

▸ Why is it especially hard when someone we love is missing on a holiday?

▸ What would have happened to Alex if he hadn't asked, "Dad, was it my fault?"

▸ **Sometimes we misunderstand something because we don't ask questions about what is happening.** Can you remember times when you were afraid to speak up and get things sorted out? What happened if you told someone how you felt?

▸ When you're afraid to talk about things that bother you, how can God help you to speak up? In what way can you take the first step? What can you say?

▸ In hard times we can hang on tight to Jesus by giving thanks for the good things we do have. Alex gave thanks for his dad's love. What are some things for which you'd like to thank God?

"The Lord himself goes before you and will be with you; he will never leave you nor forsake you. Do not be afraid; do not be discouraged." Deuteronomy 31:8

When I don't understand what is happening to me, help me ask questions, Lord. Help me talk with the people I love. Thanks that I can hang on tight to you—that you will never leave me or give up on me.

27

The Big Test

Spring sunlight warmed the room as Brian looked out the window, searching for a way to escape. Across the school yard one of his friends dropped a basketball into a hoop.

With an effort Brian turned back to his math book. "Do the two problems on page 178," Mrs. Evenson had said. Once again Brian tried to begin.

1. Meyer's Department Store is holding its annual spring sale on many items. Among them are girls' swimsuits. Some that originally sold for $25.00 are being offered at 20 percent off. Find out how much money the discount is and how much you will have to pay for the swimsuit.

Brian read on, hoping the next question would be easier.

2. Meyer's also has jeans on sale. . . .

Feeling as if his head were stuffed with cotton, Brian

drew a doodle on the side of his paper. As he forced himself to go back to number one, the tight knot in his head seemed to grow.

Percentages and discounts have always messed me up, Brian thought. *Mrs. Evenson wants us to finish before we leave today. What am I going to do?*

As though in answer to his question, the teacher went out into the hall. For a moment Brian waited, wondering how soon she would return. A minute passed. Looking to the back of the room, Brian cleared his throat. His friend Pam understood. Their gaze met and Pam nodded.

Brian stood up and walked toward her desk. On the way to the pencil sharpener, he picked up a half-folded piece of paper. After sharpening his pencil, he returned to his desk.

Within a few minutes, he had copied every answer onto his own paper. Wasting no time, Brian took another trip to the sharpener and dropped Pam's paper where it belonged.

Just as Brian returned to his desk, Mrs. Evenson came back into the room. "Everyone done?" she asked. "Let's exchange papers and correct them."

From the corner of his eye, Brian watched Carla as she marked his paper. She wrote *100* in big numbers two inches high. Beneath it, she drew a funny smiling face.

Poor Carla, thought Brian. *Doesn't she know I didn't really do it?*

Around Brian, the boys and girls passed in their math problems and cleaned off their desks. As they got ready to leave, Mrs. Evenson looked at their papers.

"Brian," she called. "Come up here, please."

His mouth dry with nervousness, Brian stood up. *Did*

Mrs. Evenson guess what I did?

The teacher held out his paper. "I'm proud of you, Brian!" she said in a voice the whole class could hear. "I know this math is difficult for you. You must have studied hard to have every question right."

Brian felt his face getting hot, but somehow he smiled. "Thanks, Mrs. Evenson," he mumbled and returned to his seat.

Whew! I made it through that one. But then another thought struck him. *What am I going to do for the test on Friday?*

TO **TALK** ABOUT

▶ What do you think will happen to Brian on Friday?

▶ What choice do you feel he should make right now? What should he do about his choice?

▶ Describe how it makes you feel when something is really hard to do. Why is it more tempting to cheat if you have trouble doing something?

▶ What have you found to be better—to take a poor grade or to cheat? Why?

▶ **To have integrity means that you are fair, honest, and strong.** If you are tempted to do something wrong, you do what is right, even if no one but you knows about it. How would it help you to be known as a person with integrity? How would you like to be known? Why?

Humble yourselves before the Lord, and he will lift you up.
James 4:10

Jesus, I heard once that humbling yourself means confessing your sins. I'm afraid to tell you about the times I've cheated, but I really am sorry about what I did. Please forgive me. Help me to have integrity—to be honest, even when it's hard.

No Longer Dark

Mei Ling flicked off the light and took a running leap into bed. Outside, the November wind blew around the corner of her room. Bare branches, stripped of leaves, scratched the side of the house. Back and forth they moved—first blocking the streetlight, then letting the light shine through.

The wavering light filled the room, sending a shiver through her whole body. Eerie shadows danced on the walls, growing long in corners and melting down into the stairway outside her door. Feeling scared and alone, Mei Ling huddled down under the blankets.

Minutes later Dad came into her room to say good-night. He gently pulled the blankets off her head. "Something wrong, Mei Ling? Can I help?"

Afraid to admit her fear of the dark, she shook her head. But Dad guessed. "Are you afraid of the wind and the dark?"

This time Mei Ling nodded.

"All of us have times when we're afraid," Dad told her. "What counts is what we do about it—like choosing to face the reason, for instance."

Going to the door, he flicked on the light switch. The bright light reached into the corners, and every shadow melted. As Mei Ling looked around the room, her fear vanished like disappearing ink.

"Now watch." Dad turned off the light and went to the window. "I can pull down the shade if you want." When he did, the room became dark with no dancing shadows. "But there's something we're missing." With a quick snap, Dad let the shade roll up. "What do you think it is?"

It was a game they had played before when Dad showed Mei Ling how to enjoy the moods of weather.

"The wildness of the November wind," she answered.

"And what is the wind doing?" Dad asked.

Mei Ling smiled. "Sending the dry, fallen leaves around to find new friends."

Dad hugged her, delighted that she remembered. "Let's read Psalm 121 tonight." Once more he turned on the light.

Mei Ling began reading, and her voice grew steadily stronger when she reached verses three and four. " 'He who watches over you will not slumber; indeed, he who watches over Israel will neither slumber nor sleep.' "

When Dad turned off the light and left, Mei Ling snuggled down under the blankets. This time she pulled them only as high as her shoulders. *It's not so bad when I face things,* she thought.

Drowsiness settled around her as she repeated Dad's verse to herself. *He who watches over me will not slumber. He will not slumber nor sleep.*

TO **TALK** ABOUT

▸ Sometimes we have a good reason to be afraid. Other times we're afraid about something we imagine. Which was it for Mei Ling?

▸ Many people are afraid of the dark. What happened when Mei Ling chose to face her fear and talk about it? What are some ways to get over a fear of the dark?

▸ Are there other things that make you afraid? Are they something real or something you imagine? Explain.

▸ Often we're afraid of things that never happen, but now and then there can be good reasons to be afraid of the weather. If a storm damages or destroys your possessions, those are things that can usually be replaced. What's really important is what happens to people. Most of the time very few people actually get hurt in a storm. If you know that severe weather is coming, how do people in your area take shelter?

▸ What does it mean to truly believe that God never sleeps? Is it fair to ask for God's protection if we are foolish in how we act?

▸ Why is God's *biggest* protection the eternal life that He gives us?

▸ **People who have courage are not people who are never afraid. People with courage have learned to act in a wise way in spite of their fear.** It may be important to think about a reason why you're afraid long enough to face it. Then ask God to help you get over that fear. Call upon Jesus by praying His name. Repeat Bible verses you've memorized. What are some verses that would help you if you're afraid?

[Jesus said,] "And surely I am with you always, to the very end of the age." Matthew 28:20

Thank you, Jesus, that when I repeat Bible verses and think about you, my fears go away. Thank you that when I'm afraid, it helps me to talk with you or my parents—not someone who scares me more. I'm glad that you've promised to be with me always.

Peace for Pete at Christmas

Pete took the stairs two at a time, tore into his bedroom, and pulled open the drawers. If he didn't hurry, he'd miss all the fun at the church party.

When he didn't find what he wanted, he yanked open the closet door. Pawing through the shelves, he threw clothes on the floor. Not there, either. Angry now, Pete kicked his wastebasket and sent it flying across the room.

Moments later he entered the kitchen. While his mother cleaned up the dishes, his little sister Janie shook sparkles on Christmas cookies and the floor.

"I can't find my red sweat shirt," Pete told his mom. "I need to leave."

"Did you wear it and forget to put it away?" she asked.

Pete thought hard. Suddenly he exploded. "*Ivan!* I bet Ivan took it. Where is he? At the play tryouts? What did he wear?"

"I know," Janie piped up. "A red sweat shirt and jeans."

"Oh, Mom, how *could* he?" Pete wailed. "Awful brother! I hate him!"

"Peter!"

"I do. I can't stand him!"

"I don't blame you for being angry," Mom said. "Ivan was wrong, but that isn't a reason to hate him. Why don't you wear something else so you don't miss the party? We'll settle the problem when you get home."

"But Ivan thinks he can take my stuff whenever he wants!"

Deep inside, Pete knew his words weren't true. Yet his anger burned hot all the way to church. Each time he thought about the sweat shirt, it was like adding wood to a bonfire.

His anger cooled as he spotted his best friends around the Christmas tree. But for the first time since he knew the church kids, the games dragged.

It's all Ivan's fault I'm not having fun, Pete decided. *How can I get even with him?*

Near the end of the evening, everyone sat down in a circle. The youth leader opened a Bible, read the first verse of the Christmas story, and handed the Bible to the person next to him. Around the circle it came, each one reading a verse.

" 'Joseph went from the town of Nazareth. . . .' "

" 'There were some shepherds in that part of the country. . . .' "

Now it was Pete's turn. The words seemed to stand out on the page. " 'Glory to God in the highest heaven, and peace on earth to those with whom he is pleased!' "*

---

*The Christmas story passages quoted here are taken from Today's English Version.

Pete stared at the verse, then passed on the Bible. But he couldn't stop thinking. *Peace on earth . . .*

Pete tried to push it aside but couldn't. *Peace on earth?*

Suddenly he felt ashamed. *Sure, Ivan did something wrong. But what about me? I've wasted the whole evening being mad at my brother.*

What should I do? Pete wondered. *Hold it over his head for the next six months? Or tell Ivan I forgive him?*

TO TALK ABOUT

▸ Do you think Pete will forgive Ivan, or will he remind Ivan about the sweat shirt every chance he gets?

▸ When Pete gets home, Mom can be referee. But why would it be better if Pete and Ivan talk with each other and settle the problem themselves?

▸ Some people say, "Forgive and forget," but it's not always easy. Why is it so hard to forget?

▸ If you forgive someone, does it always mean that person is right?

▸ **When you choose to forgive others in spite of how they hurt you, God begins to work in your own life.** Try to explain how that might happen.

▸ If a person keeps taking advantage of you by taking your things without permission, what can you do?

"If you forgive others the wrongs they have done to you, your Father in heaven will also forgive you." Matthew 6:14 (TEV)

In your strong name, Jesus, I choose to forgive the person who has hurt me. Thank you that when I forgive others, you forgive me for the wrong things I've done. Help me talk to the people who make me angry. Help us to forgive each other and solve our problems.

March Wind

As he left home, Troy felt the wind catch his jacket. It was a brisk Saturday morning in early March, and all week he had thought about launching his new rocket.

Will the wind be too strong? he wondered. Rocket under one arm and knapsack over his shoulder, he started across the large, vacant field on the edge of the city. The long grass was brown and dry, the ground hilly and uneven.

Moments later he heard Gil's shout. His friend also carried a knapsack, and Troy knew there'd be food. It would be a good day, but for an instant Troy felt uneasy. Dad didn't like it when he hung out with Gil. Twice Gil had gotten him in trouble. But Troy knew Gil liked rockets as much as he did.

If anything happens, I can always put the blame on him, Troy thought.

The two boys set to work and soon decided where to put the launch pad. Troy wanted to stay clear of the swamp and the telephone lines at the other end of the field.

Before long they had the pad in place, ready to mount

the rocket. Troy ran his hands over its smooth lines. "It's the biggest rocket I've built," he said proudly. "Bet it will go to the moon!"

Carefully he set the rocket on the launch pad. Each time Troy put a new rocket together, he looked forward to this moment. Yet he also felt the tingle of the unknown. *Will it take off?* he wondered. *Will it go the direction I want?*

As he knelt down, Gil helped steady the rocket. Troy pressed the ignition button and both of them leaped back. *Whoooosh!* Up, up, and away!

Suddenly both Troy and Gil shouted with excitement. Against the blue sky, the rocket turned and leveled out.

In the next moment, the wind caught the long, slender cone. Troy knew it was edging off course. He started to run, trying to keep the rocket in sight. Faster and faster it went—swinging toward the swamp, out above the water.

Just then Troy's foot caught a rock. He landed flat on his chest, knocking the wind out of his lungs. Unable to move, he lay there. When he tried to breathe deep, the pain got worse.

At last his breath slowly returned. With Gil's help, Troy pushed himself up to a sitting position. "What happened?" he asked when he could speak.

"To the rocket? I'm not sure."

"Did you see it land in the swamp?"

"Yup." Gil looked gloomy. "It couldn't have gone in a worse place."

As soon as Troy could walk, they headed toward the spot where they'd last seen the rocket. When he reached soft ground, Troy tried to step on clumps of grass. Instead, he slipped into the cold water. Gil tried another place and went in up to his knees.

After a long search, they had to give up. By then both of them were shivering.

"Let's build a fire," Gil said.

"No way," answered Troy. "We're not supposed to."

"But I've got marshmallows. We could roast them."

It wasn't hard for Troy to remember how toasted marshmallows tasted. He was tempted. Except for that brief moment of the rocket's flight, the day had been a zero.

Then he remembered Dad's words: *"Never, never start a fire in that field."*

Dad's right, thought Troy. The field around the swamp was really dry.

"See that spot over by that rock?" asked Gil. "It's not as windy there. We could sit close to the fire and warm up."

Troy shook his head. "Dad said no fire."

But Gil paid no attention. "Just a minute. I'll get what we need."

Moments later he was back with two sticks for the marshmallows and some dried-out branches for kindling.

Troy had to admit it would feel good to warm up. Already he could taste the marshmallows. Just the thought of their soft, creamy center tempted him. Troy helped Gil carry the wood over to the sheltered place between the rocks.

Pushing his uneasiness aside, Troy tried to ignore the nudge of his conscience. "We've got to keep the fire small."

"We will," Gil promised.

"If anything happens, it's your fault," said Troy.

Gil stared at him. "My fault! What do you mean, my fault?"

"It's your idea, and you know it!"

"Hey, you're in this, too! You can't put the blame on me!"

Troy still felt uneasy, but Gil had the bag of marshmallows out. Pulling up clumps, he laid the long, dry grass in a heap. Then he put the small branches on top and lit the grass. Seconds later the fire caught.

It had just flared up when a gust of wind circled the rocks. Catching the flames, the wind pushed them toward the long grass nearby. Afraid now, Troy jumped to his feet.

"Hey, it's all right," Gil said. "Nothing will happen."

But fingers of flame reached out, beginning to crawl. Troy pulled off his jacket and beat it against the flames. He tried hard but couldn't keep up.

A moment later the wind swung around. One small flame from the other side of the campfire reached out, grabbed more grass, and devoured it.

This time Gil jumped up. Already the fire was moving away, eating whatever it touched. "Run!" he shouted.

Troy still pounded his jacket on the ground, trying to get the fire out. But the wind changed again, and the fire started off in a new direction. "It's headed toward the houses! Gil, help me!"

"It's too late! Let's get out of here!"

Grabbing their knapsacks, the two boys took off toward the houses. Soon they reached a garage.

"Hide!" Gil found an unlocked door, and they stumbled inside. For a moment they stood there, gasping and catching their breath.

"We've gotta tell someone!" Troy cried. "We've gotta call the fire department!"

"Not on your life!" Gil said.

"But the people in the houses!" More than Troy's conscience hurt him now. With terror he thought about what could happen. "We have to warn them!"

"We gotta get out of here, you mean!" Gil exclaimed. "We're too close to the fire!"

Fleeing the garage, they rounded the corner and raced down the street. Just then a fire engine wailed in the distance.

"Someone must have called 9-1-1!" Troy was panting now. "They'll get the fire out."

Deep inside he felt relieved. At the same time, his terror had changed to panic. *I just need to get home in time to cover my tracks.*

Stretching out his legs, Troy ran with a speed he didn't know he had. *If I lie about where I've been, I'll be able to wiggle my way out of everything.*

TO **TALK** ABOUT

▸ What do you think will happen? Do you believe Troy will be able to wiggle his way out of trouble? Why or why not?

▸ Whose fault was it that the fire started? Explain.

▸ It may seem like a good idea to blame someone else to keep out of trouble. Yet blaming others can hurt us. What do you think will happen to Troy if he puts the blame on Gil and gets away with it?

▸ **God created us with a conscience to help us recognize the difference between right and wrong.** If we say no to our conscience about the wrong things we do, we hide sin in our heart. What will happen to Troy if he keeps saying no to his conscience? How will it hurt any relationship he might have with God?

▸ **Trust is built by people who tell and live the truth.** Why is it important that you are able to trust other people? Why is it important that other people are able to trust you?

▸ Why is it very difficult to trust a liar?

▸ Who is the most truthful person who ever lived? How do you know?

I have hidden your word in my heart that I might not sin against you. Psalm 119:11

Jesus answered, "I am the way and the truth and the life. No one comes to the Father except through me." John 14:6

Forgive me, Jesus, for the wrong things I've done— especially the things I seem to have gotten away with. If I need to own up to anything, help me to set things right. Give me the power of your Holy Spirit to be truthful in everything I do.

Just a Minute, Mom

Mr. Alvarez stopped Mick on the way to his desk. "I want to talk with you."

Mick's breath caught. *Here it comes*, he thought. *Just what I've been dreading.*

The teacher opened his grade book. "Your work is good, but when I assign something to be done outside of class, you always hand it in late. It's just as hard to do it later on, and I have to give you a lower grade. Why don't you get it in on time?"

Mick looked down. How could he tell Mr. Alvarez that he hated homework so much that he always put it off?

After a long moment of silence, Mr. Alvarez spoke again. "You're forming a habit that will hurt you the rest of your life. I'll have to talk to your mother."

Mick's head jerked up. "Oh, don't do that."

"I don't have any choice. You need to learn responsibility."

That afternoon Mick dreaded going home. He didn't want to add something more to the load his mom already carried as a single parent. Yet Mick didn't know how to change things, either. What would Mom say?

As he watched a video in the family room, his mother came home. Through the door into the kitchen, Mick saw the groceries she carried, but he didn't get up.

As she brought in the third bag, his mother asked, "Can you help me put these away, Mick?"

"Just a minute, Mom," he answered, his gaze on the TV again.

The heavy thud of a bag on the counter caught Mick's attention. His mother's shoulders sagged even more than usual. When she moved between the sink and fridge, she looked tired.

A twinge of shame touched him, and Mick dragged himself to his feet. As he put away the groceries, he noticed the lines around his mother's eyes. "You okay, Mom?" he asked.

"No, I'm not." His mother dropped onto a kitchen chair. "I keep getting longer and harder reports at work. At least I finished the worst one so I don't have to figure it out tomorrow."

She pushed a strand of hair out of her eyes. "When I get something I don't like to do, I tell myself, 'Do it first. Get it behind you.' And I did."

But her look of discouragement deepened. "Mr. Alvarez called me at work, Mick. I'm disappointed with you. You're having the same problem both here and at school. I wish you'd change your pattern of putting things off."

"Aw, Mom," Mick answered. "I just don't feel like doing homework after I've been in school all day. And I don't feel like doing stuff around here."

His mother stood up. "Come to think of it, I don't feel like making your supper, either. I'll be back in a bit."

A few minutes later, Mick heard the car start and knew he was in big trouble. What could be worse than having to fix his own supper?

When he went to the fridge for leftovers, Mick found gray fur growing in the first bowl of food he opened. The second container held a combination of veggies he wouldn't eat unless stranded on a desert island. The third dish looked downright appetizing. In fact, it was one of his favorite hot dishes. But Mick soon discovered he didn't know how to start the microwave.

After pushing buttons for a time, he decided to eat the food cold. When he gagged on that, he rounded out his meal with three bowls of cereal.

By now the kitchen looked like a war zone. Mick had no doubt that he should clean it up. Instead, he dropped down in front of the TV.

"Shut it off," Mom said when she returned. "First do the dishes. Then your homework."

Again Mick dragged himself up. As he started to rinse off the dishes, Mom poked her head into the kitchen.

"I'm going to bed early," she said. "And I'm not going to nag anymore. From now on it's up to you."

As soon as she closed her bedroom door, Mick went back to the TV. He found the show even better than usual, but he kept hearing a tape of Mr. Alvarez's voice. *"You're forming a habit that will hurt you . . . hurt you . . . hurt you."* Each time the thought returned, Mick pushed it away. When the program ended, he switched channels. Three hours later he fell asleep in front of the TV.

Early morning light wakened him. Cold and stiff from lying on the sofa without a blanket, Mick remembered his homework and the dirty dishes. *Oh no! I'll get it now!*

Panic clutched him. *Why do I always do this? The dishes will be twice as hard to wash. Mr. Alvarez will chew me out again.*

As Mick sat up, his dread deepened. *I hate myself for not getting things done. But how do I change?*

Like a song going around in his head, he remembered his mother's words: *"Do it first. Get it behind you."* Mick glanced at the clock. He still had an hour before he needed to leave for school.

Should I do my homework or clean up the kitchen? Or should I crawl into bed?

Mick yawned three times, then dug in. By the time he finished the dishes, he felt surprised at himself. As he hung the dishcloth over the faucet, he grinned. *I bet Mom will faint with surprise when she sees this.*

TO **TALK** ABOUT

▸ How can TV or a video offer something good? How can it be an excuse to put things off? In which way do you use the TV or videos?

▸ What do you think will be some good consequences of Mick's new beginning?

▸ Is it easier to wait to do something, or to do it right away? How do you know?

‣ What does it mean to take responsibility for doing something? Give an example from your own life.

‣ Describe someone who has been a responsible, trustworthy person in your life. What do you like best about that person? Why does he or she make you feel that way?

‣ How does God use little tests to train us to be responsible? Though even little tests can be hard, do you sometimes feel glad for them? Why?

When I'm tempted to put things off, help me, Lord. I want to be a person others can trust. Help me form good habits so you can use me in the plans you have for me. Thank you!

"For I know the plans I have for you," declares the Lord, "plans to prosper you and not to harm you, plans to give you hope and a future." Jeremiah 29:11

I Dare You!

Kelsey yawned and looked up at the hands of the clock. With a new boy in school, it had been an exciting day. Yet now time seemed to have stopped.

Finally the hands moved on, minute by minute. Kelsey couldn't wait to be out for the day, free as a breeze.

Jill, the most popular girl in the room, had chosen her, Kelsey. Nina, the second most popular girl, was coming along. Sure, it was longer to walk home the way they chose, but it would be worth it.

At last the moment came. Surrounded by a hundred other kids, they pushed their way out the school door and started down the street. Soon they left the others behind.

Jill giggled. "Don't you like the new boy? I just love Rob's brown eyes. And his muscles—*wow!*" She tossed her head, and her blond hair swung around her shoulders. "Did you see the way Rob watches me? I'm sure he likes me."

Sure that clouds had moved across the sun, Kelsey glanced up. But nothing had changed. Twice Rob had spoken to her that morning. When they traded test papers, he smiled at the funny mark Kelsey used for corrections. He liked the cartoon she drew at the bottom. She had wondered, *Could he really like me?* But now Jill said . . .

Kelsey ached inside. *How can I make Rob like me? What can I do to be as popular as Jill?*

Just then Jill opened her book bag. "Look! I've got half a pack of cigarettes my mom left out. Let's cut down this street, and no one will see us."

Kelsey stopped in her tracks. "No, I don't think so."

"Oh, come on," Jill said. "I've smoked before, and it's really neat."

"I've tried it, too," Nina joined in. "It won't hurt you any."

"Then why do they put that warning on cigarettes?" Kelsey asked.

"That's just for people who aren't strong," answered Jill. "Nothing will happen to you."

"Sorry," Kelsey said. "I know people who can't stop smoking. I don't want to start."

"Are you kidding?" Jill asked. "You'll never be popular that way!"

"You're just a scaredy-cat," Nina said. "I dare you to give it a try."

Kelsey cringed. Her mixed-up feelings seemed like a waterfall tumbling over rocks. "I *like* you!" she wanted to cry out. "I don't want you dying of lung cancer the way my uncle did!" But the words stuck in her throat.

She wondered if Jill and Nina could see that her face felt hot with embarrassment. *Is this what it means to be popular? If I say no, does it mean I can't be their friend?*

TO **TALK** ABOUT

▸ What do you think Kelsey will do? If she keeps saying no to cigarettes, what do you think Jill and Nina will do?

▸ Is it important to be popular with everyone? Why or why not? Do you think God sometimes wants us to be *unpopular*? Give some reasons for your answer.

▸ The nicotine used in cigarettes is a poisonous substance that is used to kill insects. Nicotine can also cause smokers to become addicted. What does it mean to start a bad habit that might lead to *addiction*?

▸ It can be your protection that you don't feel at home with every group. What is a bad consequence of choosing to be in the wrong group? Why is it important to know that?

▸ **The Bible shows us how God wants us to live.** If you're tempted to do something wrong, how can the Bible verses you've memorized help you make the right choice? How did Jesus use Bible verses when He was tempted? Big clue: See Luke 4:1–13.

"Don't be afraid! Stand your ground, and you will see what the Lord will do to save you today." Exodus 14:13 (TEV)

When I'm tempted to do wrong, help me to say no, Jesus, even if I'm scared. Help me to stand my ground. To answer in such a way that kids know I mean NO! Thank you that I don't have to choose wrong things in order to be popular.

Never Good Enough

I'm afraid to see my report card, thought Molly. *I've never worked so hard in my life. If my grades aren't better, I'll feel like giving up.*

A moment later the teacher stopped by Molly's desk, and her warm smile offered hope. As she saw her grades, Molly wanted to shout. She could barely keep the good news inside.

Walking home, Molly hugged her best friend. "Wow! Do you know what? I got three *B*s and one *A*. I've never done so well. I can't believe it!"

Alycia hugged her back. "You studied hard, Molly. You earned those grades. I'm proud of you!"

A warm feeling of satisfaction filled Molly till she felt like a soda can ready to fizz over. The feeling stayed with her as she reached the house and found her mom home early from work. But when she walked into the kitchen, Molly discovered things were not going well for her mother.

"Hi, Molly," she said. "Put away your things, okay? Fischers will be here in two hours."

"Sure, Mom, but I want to show you my grades."

"Not right now. I have to get this meat in the oven and the veggies ready and the table set."

"But, Mom, it just takes a minute. I want you to see what I got—three *B*s and one *A*!"

"That's nice, Molly. Now go clean the bathroom for me. When you're done with that, vacuum the hall."

Molly walked slowly to her bedroom. Some of the fizz had gone out of her day. All that work, and Mom hadn't even heard what she said. Well, maybe Dad would be interested.

As Molly finished vacuuming, her dad came in. "Hi, pumpkin," he said with a quick hug.

As he headed down the hall, Molly stopped him. "I got my grades today, Dad. I think you'll like them. I worked as hard as I could, just like you said."

Dad waited while Molly got her report card. "See? Isn't that great?"

"Hmm," Dad said.

Molly anxiously watched his face. *I just want to know that he cares. If he likes what I did, all the work will be worth it.*

"Hmm," Dad said again. Then he looked up. "I bet if you had really tried you could have gotten all *A*s."

The can of pop inside Molly fizzed out. Taking the report card, she walked to her bedroom without another word. Though she blinked away tears, Dad didn't seem to notice.

Once she was alone, the torrent came. "Oh, God!" Molly cried out. "I wanted them to be proud of me! I tried so hard. But I studied and studied, and it wasn't enough! Whatever I do, it's never good enough!"

Molly's shoulders shook as she cried into her pillow so Mom and Dad wouldn't hear. Like a bike wheel spinning very fast, the words went round and round in her head. "Not good enough. Not good enough. Not good enough."

Finally Molly blew her nose. *Should I stop trying? Should I give up? What's the use?*

Then from deep inside came a memory. Her friend Alycia had said, *"I'm proud of you!"* And once, she had said something more. *"God is proud of you, too!"*

A new thought came to Molly. *Jesus, you know I really tried, don't you? What do you think about my grades? Are they good enough for you?*

Molly felt sure she knew the answer.

TO **TALK** ABOUT

▸ If you could talk to Molly about her three *B*s and one *A*, what would you say? Do you think it would help Molly to show her report card again later when her mom isn't so busy?

▸ Molly knows she has done her best. What is more important—the sense of satisfaction she feels about her grades or how someone else reacts? Why do you think so?

▸ Why does it mean so much to have the approval of our parents or others close to us?

▸ What do you suppose God thinks about the work Molly did? How can she choose to focus on that?

▸ Even if we don't receive praise or an outward reward, it's important that we know we did something well. Describe something that you have learned to do well.

"The Lord your God is with you, he is mighty to save. He will take great delight in you, he will quiet you with his love, he will rejoice over you with singing." Zephaniah 3:17

Jesus, it means so much to me when the people I love tell me I'm doing great. If they don't encourage me, help me to be glad when I've done my best. I'm grateful that you care about me and everything I do. Thank you that you even delight in me! That you're glad for who I am!

Libby Comes to Bat

"Let's go to the baseball diamond at the park," Libby said.

"Let's not and say we did," answered Kai as he tossed a softball in the air.

Libby tried again. "My dad said we're not supposed to play in the street."

"Aw, c'mon, Libby, the park is too far away," Kai told her.

Libby still had her doubts. After all, she was the one with the most to lose. She lived here, while the others came from blocks farther away.

"Hey, Libby, do you wanna play or don't ya?" called another boy.

"Well . . ." Libby started to give in. "Put first base a few more feet that way." She pointed along the curb. "Mrs. O'Rourke is crabby. She doesn't want us on her grass."

They moved first base onto another neighbor's lawn and started playing. Soon Libby came up to bat.

Kai was pitching, and Libby knew he'd give her his fastest ball. Taking a firm grip on the bat, she waited. Sure enough, there it came—a little low, but right over the plate.

Libby swung and connected. A fly popped off to the right. Then *C-R-A-A-A-S-S-H!* The sound of broken glass shattered the air.

Libby looked around and felt sick. Sure enough, it was Mrs. O'Rourke's window.

One moment everyone stared at the house. The next instant every kid scattered in a different direction.

Every kid, that is, except Libby. She felt frozen to the spot. Then, as she recovered, she headed for the bushes across the street. Just in time she knelt down, hiding behind the leaves and peering through.

Mrs. O'Rourke opened her front door. Cane in hand, she came out on the porch. With her white hair piled on top of her head, she looked slender and tall. But Libby knew it was difficult for her to walk. Today she leaned on her cane more than usual.

Mrs. O'Rourke looked at the shattered glass, then turned to the empty street. Her face crumpled.

It doesn't matter, Libby told herself, trying to ignore the woman's hurt look. Hiding behind the bushes, Libby knew she could get away. *Mrs. O'Rourke might guess, but she can't prove I did it. After all, a lot of kids were here.*

Then the older woman moved, and her cane slipped on the glass. Still Libby waited, afraid that Mrs. O'Rourke would be mad.

Why should I take the blame? Libby asked herself. *All the kids were in on it!*

As she watched, Mrs. O'Rourke stretched out her cane, and her feet followed. Slowly she went back into the house.

Libby backed away from the bushes that hid her. On her hands and knees, she crept to the corner of the nearby house. But instead of edging away to safety, she waited a minute.

Everything within Libby wanted to run. At the same time, something held her there. Most of all, she felt ashamed.

Finally Libby stood up. Feeling as if her legs were not her own, she walked into the open. As she crossed the street, her feet dragged. Just the same, Libby climbed the steps and rang the bell.

I'm crazy for doing this, she thought as she waited. *All the other kids will get away free!*

When Mrs. O'Rourke opened the screen door, Libby waited for the angry words she thought she'd hear. Instead, Mrs. O'Rourke spoke quietly.

"Hello, Libby."

Libby looked down at the weather-beaten porch. The boards were gray with time, and Libby wondered if other kids had ever stood where she did. Then she looked up into Mrs. O'Rourke's faded blue eyes.

"I'm sorry," she said. She wanted to tell Mrs. O'Rourke that it wasn't her fault. She wanted to put the blame on the other kids. But only four words came out. "I broke your window."

"I know," Mrs. O'Rourke surprised Libby by saying. "Just before the ball hit, I saw you out another window. I was going to call your dad at his office."

Libby's gaze fell to the old boards once more. Panic filled

her now. *What if she'd been standing at the window I broke?*

Full of misery, Libby apologized again. "I'm sorry. *Really* sorry. I'm glad you weren't hurt."

"I forgive you," Mrs. O'Rourke answered quietly. "I respect you for coming to talk with me. I know that was hard to do."

Suddenly Libby's gaze found the older woman's eyes. Something Libby saw there drew her to Mrs. O'Rourke. *Why have I always thought she's crabby?* Libby wondered.

Aloud she asked, "What can I do to pay for the window?"

Mrs. O'Rourke swung the screen door farther open. "Why don't you come in? We'll talk about it."

Libby drew a deep breath. For some strange reason, she almost felt as if she had a new friend.

TO **TALK** ABOUT

▸ **When you make good or bad choices, there are logical consequences.** For Libby and the other kids, what was a bad choice? What were the consequences?

▸ The story tells some of the feelings Libby had about the broken window. Give some of the feelings you have when you do something wrong and don't want to own up to it.

▸ Libby also made some good choices that had good consequences. Instead of running away, she went to Mrs. O'Rourke. When she apologized she said, "I'm sorry." Sometimes people are just sorry that they got caught, not for what they did wrong. Which way did Libby feel? How do you know?

▸ Libby was also very direct. She said, "I broke your window," instead of putting the blame on other kids. Compare what Libby did with the way Troy thought he would wiggle his way out of trouble. (See "March Wind," p. 41.) Who do you respect more? Why?

▸ Mrs. O'Rourke did some special things for Libby. What were they? Why is it important that Mrs. O'Rourke said, "I forgive you"?

▸ Libby saw the hurt she caused and said she was wrong. She also understood there was a consequence for what she did. What do you suppose Libby and Mrs. O'Rourke decided about the broken window? What would you do if you were Libby?

Jesus, when I've done something wrong, help me do the right thing to correct it. Help me own up to what I did and deal with the consequences. Thank you that when-ever I ask forgiveness, you do forgive me.

For the Lord God is a sun and shield; the Lord will give grace and glory; No good thing will He withhold from those who walk uprightly. Psalm 84:11 (NKJV)

The New Baby

When Justin went to the hospital to see his new baby brother, it was fun. "Here he is!" said Dad, putting the blanket-wrapped bundle in Justin's arms. "Your little brother, Daniel!"

"He looks just like you did," Mom said.

Justin's friend Adam had told him all about new babies. But Justin couldn't see much of this one—only the blanket, a shock of hair, and a tiny face. The sleeping baby didn't seem like a brother at all.

"He's so *little*!" Justin exclaimed.

"Yup, he is," answered Dad. "But he'll grow fast. Before you know it, you'll be able to toss a ball to him."

Justin doubted it, but just then the baby yawned and opened his eyes. Mom pulled the blanket aside so Justin could see Daniel's arms and legs. As he waved a little fist, he looked like he was saying hi.

Justin laughed at the weird expression on Daniel's face. "Did I really look like that? His skin is so red and wrinkly."

But when Mom brought Daniel home from the hospital,

Justin discovered it wasn't quite so much fun. Often the baby cried at night. Sometimes he woke Justin up. Then there was the company! Everyone brought a present and gathered around the baby to *ooh* and *ahh*.

"All that red hair!" said one lady. "What a good-looking boy!"

My little brother is good-looking? Justin asked himself. He didn't dare say what he really thought.

But in the week that followed, everyone agreed with the lady. Not only was Daniel good-looking. Not only did he have lots of red hair. He was also the perfect weight, the perfect size, and the perfect baby! Everyone talked only about Daniel.

Then one day Aunt Meg and several of Mom's friends came over. When Mom brought out Daniel, they passed him from one person to another. By that time Justin had seen enough.

Oooh! Ahhh! he told himself, growing more and more angry. Justin felt left out and decided to hunt up his friend Adam.

As Justin headed for the door, one of the ladies asked, "Isn't Daniel a nice brother?" But she went on talking before Justin could answer.

Then Aunt Meg spotted him. "Hi, Justin! What have you been doing lately?"

Usually Justin liked Aunt Meg, but today he didn't feel like talking to anyone. When he managed to slip outside, he took his bike from the garage and went for a ride. Along the way he found Adam.

Justin didn't want to tell how he felt, but he was so quiet

that Adam guessed. He tried to comfort Justin.

"That's the way grown-ups act about a new baby. They'll be over it soon. I should know."

Adam would know, all right. With three younger sisters, he was an expert on babies.

"And you don't need to feel jealous," Adam went on. "I used to. But look at all the stuff I can do that my sisters can't. They just have to be around Mom all the time."

Justin was starting to feel better. But he still didn't like the way his life had changed.

When he finally returned home, Mom asked, "Where have you been? Aunt Meg wanted to talk with you more, but we couldn't find you."

Mom looked tired as she stood by the stove, jiggling the baby in one arm. With her other hand, she stirred the stew for supper. Daniel yowled.

Justin remembered the days when Mom always seemed bouncy. She hadn't looked bouncy for a long time. Right now she looked as if she wanted to cry along with Daniel.

For the first time, Justin wondered about something. "Mom?" he asked. "Is it sometimes hard for you to have Daniel?"

Mom looked thoughtful. "Yes, I guess I'd have to say that sometimes it is."

"Was it ever hard for you to have me?"

"Yes, sometimes it was. But I loved you so much it was worth it." She grinned. "Don't you agree? You turned out really well!" Leaving the stove, she gave Justin a hug with her free arm.

In that moment something broke loose inside Justin.

Something that had been hurting ever since the baby came home. He felt strange—almost free again—as if he'd been let out of school for summer vacation.

Since that day in the hospital, Justin hadn't held Daniel. He hadn't wanted to. Now he felt surprised by his own words. "Do you want me to hold him?"

This time Mom's smile reached her eyes. As soon as Justin sat down, she put the baby on his lap.

In that instant Daniel looked up and stopped crying. He seemed to check Justin out.

At first Justin felt afraid to move. He just felt glad that Daniel seemed to like him. Then, after a few minutes, Justin decided to try something. With one finger he rubbed the palm of Daniel's hand, the way he'd seen Mom do. Daniel's little fingers closed around Justin's bigger one. Then the baby's lips parted and curved up at the corners.

"Hey, he smiled!" Justin exclaimed.

"Sure enough!" Mom said. "That's his first smile. And he gave it to you!"

Justin leaned back in the chair and made himself comfortable. *Maybe it won't be so bad having a brother after all!*

TO **TALK** ABOUT

▶ At first Justin felt jealous of his little brother. How did feeling jealous change the way Justin acted toward Daniel?

▶ What good things happened because Justin chose to see his mom and baby brother in a new way?

‣ Justin talked to Adam, but he didn't tell his mom or dad how he felt about the new baby. One way he could start would be to say, "I feel" and finish the sentence with a word that describes his feelings. He could say glad, sad, mad, or whatever he felt. What do you think Justin could have told his mom?

‣ Do you think Justin's mom guessed his feelings? Why is it important for her to know what he's thinking?

‣ **If you have jealous or angry feelings, it doesn't mean you're a bad person. What's important is what you do about your feelings.** A good place to start is to talk about them. You can use words that Justin needed—"I feel glad, or sad, or mad." When you talk to the right person, it helps you sort things out. What people in your life can you talk to? How can they help you feel better?

‣ **When you talk about things that bother you, you will usually find new ways to solve a problem.** Think about a problem in your life. What is it? Find the right person and start talking!

that I feel much better.
Thank you that when I do, I get things sorted out. Thanks
help me talk about my feelings with the right person.
Jesus, sometimes I'm all mixed up. When I feel that way,

riches in Christ Jesus. Philippians 4:19
My God will meet all your needs according to his glorious

Jennifer's Special Friend

Jennifer felt nervous as she entered the long hallway. Since moving to a new school, she had dreaded Monday mornings. It seemed everyone had plenty to talk about. Everyone had a special friend. Everyone belonged to a group.

Everyone, that is, except me, thought Jennifer.

Already a cluster of girls had formed around Dena's locker. Jennifer knew they'd be talking about all that had happened that weekend. She wished she could join them. It'd be fun to listen even if she didn't have much to say.

At the same time, Jennifer felt afraid to walk past them. They all seemed very sure of themselves and often made her feel shut out. Yet her locker was a short way down the hall beyond Dena's.

Maybe someone will notice my new jacket, Jennifer thought, remembering how great she had looked when she dressed that morning. *Maybe they'll think I'm worth having in their group.*

A tiny spark of hope came to life. *There's Ellie. She knows me. She'll say hi.*

Trying to look more confident than she felt, Jennifer drew a deep breath. *If I smile, they have to smile back.* But even as the thought came, she started feeling shaky inside.

As Jennifer neared the girls, Ellie looked up. Jennifer stopped. "Hi, Ellie," she said, the words feeling stiff on her lips.

For a moment she thought Ellie would answer. Instead, she raised her chin slightly and turned back to the others. All the girls laughed.

Jennifer felt the hot blush of embarrassment rush to her face. She wanted to run but seemed frozen to the spot. Somehow she put one foot in front of the other. *Were they laughing at me? Or just trying to make me feel left out?*

Either way, Jennifer knew it made no difference. Instead of going to her locker, she headed for the bathroom.

To her relief it was empty. She'd been spending a lot of time there. She knew every crack in the floor, every faucet that didn't quite turn off. She wished she could hide there forever.

Dropping her books on a ledge, Jennifer went to the mirror. Somehow her new jacket didn't seem nearly as nice as it had earlier that day. She felt the material and tried to believe it was still important. It wasn't. Instead, the mirror reflected the tears in her brown eyes.

Jennifer blinked the tears away, but her lips trembled. *I'm not going to cry,* she promised herself. The loneliness she felt was too deep. On days like this, it seemed the ache would never go away. *It's no use. They'll never accept me.*

I'll never be part of their group.

It wasn't the first time Jennifer had prayed, but now she meant business. *Jesus, help me. I don't know what to do. I forgive them, but I feel worthless. I need friends.*

In that moment the bell rang. Jennifer picked up her books and walked out slowly, dreading the hours ahead.

As the days passed, Jennifer wondered if God would answer her prayer. Nothing seemed to change. The girls who gathered at Dena's locker still laughed or looked away when she passed. Jennifer pasted a smile on her face, but she no longer tried to say hi. She knew it was no use.

Then one Monday when Jennifer walked past the girls, she had the strangest feeling—as though she didn't walk alone.

Not quite sure what had happened, Jennifer thought about it. *Nothing's changed.*

A moment later she realized that wasn't true. *I forgave them, didn't I? Is that what made the difference?*

Standing by her locker, Jennifer tried to figure it out. *It felt like an invisible bubble around me. Their meanness didn't get through.*

As though a light had gone on in her mind, she remembered Jesus and His long walk to the cross. She knew who had walked with her.

For the first time, Jennifer saw the girls as they really were. Her thoughts exploded. *I don't need a bunch of stuck-up friends! I don't need kids who just think about clothes!*

In that instant Jennifer felt like a different person. She

knew she had made a big discovery. *It's their problem, not mine!*

Jennifer wanted to shout it out to the whole world. *Wow! Why did it take me so long to figure that out?* Then she had another thought. *If that's the way they treat me, what do they do to other kids? Are they mean to everyone outside their group?*

It didn't take long to find out. On Wednesday a new girl named Haley started school. Dena and her friends gave Haley the same treatment.

But now Jennifer knew what to do. She felt good about trying. *I'll start by making friends with Haley.*

And she did.

to **TALK** about

▸ Sometimes kids think they show power by shutting other kids out. How was Jennifer shut out by the "in" group? What do you think of a group that treats someone that way?

▸ How does it feel to be shut out? Can you think of a time when you were shut out or when you shut out someone else? What happened?

▸ When people hurt us, we don't have to wait until we feel good about them or like what they're doing before we forgive them. That might never happen! But **forgiveness gives us a way to stop hurting.** Jennifer chose to forgive Dena's group by praying, "Jesus, I forgive them." After her prayer, what changes did God bring?

> What was Jennifer's big discovery? How can you use her discovery to fix something hard in your life? What do you think is more important—the clothes you have or how you treat others? Why?

> Why does Jesus understand when we feel lonely and left out? For clues read Isaiah 53, a chapter that tells what would happen to Jesus hundreds of years later.

> **God always hears our prayers. Yet He may not suddenly make everything right in the way we hope.** Instead, He might give us a sense of being loved or change how we feel about what's happening. Have you felt Jesus with you in one of those ways? How has He helped you accept something hard, even though you didn't like it? What happened?

> Jesus loves you, even if you can't "feel" that He does. How do you *know* that He loves you?

[Jesus said,] "I will never turn away anyone who comes to me." John 6:37b (TEV)

Jesus, I don't like feeling lonely and left out. But I forgive the kids who make me feel that way. I'm glad that you will never turn me away. Thanks for always loving me. Help me know deep inside that you do.

Curious Kate

On the bus ride to her friend's house, Kate took a good look at Shelly. *Something's wrong,* Kate decided. *Shelly is changing.*

The change bothered Kate. Since kindergarten the two had been good friends. Even on that first day of school they had ridden the bus together. But now Kate didn't understand what was happening. *We're both growing up, but it's not that. With Shelly it's something more.*

When Shelly laughed it didn't reach her eyes. Instead, the laugh that was once full of fun had a hard ring to it.

Kate twisted the end of her long black braid, thinking about it. Kate couldn't understand why Shelly was changing.

For a moment she stared out the window, but she was really praying. *Jesus, I care about my friend. Will you show me what's wrong?*

When their bus squealed to a stop, Kate and Shelly climbed down and walked to the house. In the kitchen they found Shelly's dad sitting at the table with a snack.

"Hi, Shelly. Hi, Kate. Have a good day?"

Shelly shrugged.

"How did your test go?" her dad asked.

"Same as always." Shelly's dark eyes were angry. Turning her back to her dad, she seemed to say, *What's it to you?*

Her dad started to speak, then stopped, as if wanting to wait until Kate wasn't there. Instead, he offered them food. But Shelly shook her head.

Did they have a fight? Kate wondered. She doubted it. If they had, Shelly's dad would have done his best to straighten it out before she left in the morning. Now his eyes looked as troubled as Kate felt.

Without another word Shelly headed down the steps to her bedroom in the basement. From long practice Kate knew where to find the munchies. Goodies in hand, Kate followed her friend to her room.

Already Shelly had headphones clapped around her head, listening to a CD. As she swayed with the music, Kate dropped down on the floor and started eating.

Before long, Shelly ripped off the headphones and held out the CD player. "Listen up! You'll like it!"

Even before Kate slipped the headphones over her ears, she heard and felt the heavy beat of the bass. Shelly dropped down on her bed, but her foot still moved in time to the music.

For a few minutes Kate listened, but she was unable to hear the words. When she turned down the sound, it made no difference. The words were still a muddle.

Lying on her back, hands behind her head, Shelly stared up at a poster on her ceiling.

Kate's gaze followed hers. More than the picture in the

poster, Kate caught the feel of it—the darkness. She couldn't explain what was wrong. She only knew that the poster made her uneasy. "Where did you get it?" she asked.

"Guy at school," Shelly told her. "He loaned me a bunch of CDs, too." She motioned to a pile of them.

Still trying to hear the words, Kate picked up the nearest case and pulled out the paper. As she read the lyrics, she heard beyond the strong beat and started picking out the words. The longer she listened and read, the more sick she felt.

My best friend likes this? The words of the song were exactly opposite of everything Jesus wanted them to be. *What am I going to say to her?*

Then Kate remembered to pray without closing her eyes. When she finished she drew a deep breath. As she flipped her long braid over her shoulder, she knew where to start.

"Shelly, we've been good friends for a long time. Remember what we promised each other? That we'd tell each other stuff, even if it's hard?"

Shelly pushed herself up to look at Kate. When Shelly nodded, Kate began. "Do you know what the words of these songs really say?"

TO TALK ABOUT

▸ Kate could have just shrugged her shoulders and decided the message in the CDs didn't matter. Why was it important for her to be honest?

▸ **Whatever we allow into our bodies through our eyes, ears, mouth, emotions, mind, or spirit be-**

comes part of us. How had the music already become part of Shelly? In what ways had she changed?

▶ How do you think Shelly answered Kate? What do you think Shelly will do about what Kate says?

▶ What would you do? Why?

Whatever is true, whatever is noble, whatever is right, whatever is pure, whatever is lovely, whatever is admirable—if anything is excellent or praiseworthy—think about such things. Philippians 4:8

Protect me, Jesus, from harmful thoughts that would enter my mind through what I see, hear, and read. I want to think about the good things that are true and noble and right and pure and lovely. Most of all, I want to think about you. Help me to be strong in you. Help me to help others grow strong in you.

D.J. and
the Bully

D.J. glanced over his shoulder. *Uh-oh*, he thought. Not far behind in the crowded school hallway, Eddie was moving up, all 150 pounds of him. Even from this distance, D.J. could hear him laugh with his buddy Teo.

D.J. turned toward his locker and pretended he didn't see. Clutching his books under one arm, he started twirling the combination lock. *I hate that big bully,* he thought.

It wasn't hard to remember how Eddie had kicked him in the leg. D.J. still felt sore. And his face grew hot with embarrassment just thinking about another time. In front of all the kids, Eddie had teased him about a T-shirt he wore.

Maybe Eddie won't notice me this time, D.J. thought.

The next moment he felt a jolt from behind. His books flew out from beneath his arm. Papers scattered in every direction.

D.J. whirled to face Eddie. "You big bully!" he shouted. "Who do you think you are?"

Eddie moved forward, his face mean. But D.J. held his ground.

Just then Teo stepped between them. "Hey, Eddie, what'cha do that for?"

"The fun of it," answered the bigger boy. "Just to watch the splatter. Pretty good, huh?"

"Pretty stupid," Teo said. "Some fun. C'mon. Forget it."

They moved off down the hall, and D.J. felt relieved. Yet he also felt worthless, like a clod of dirt beneath Eddie's feet.

As D.J. picked up his books and papers, the anger within him grew. That anger still burned at suppertime when he told Mom and Dad what happened.

"Eddie?" Mom asked. "Does he have any friends?"

"Teo," D.J. told her. "But even Teo didn't like him today."

"Eddie sounds like a very unhappy person," said Dad.

"Well . . . I guess I never thought about it. I just know I can't stand him."

"If even his friend doesn't like the way he acts, what does Eddie do for fun?" asked Dad.

"I don't know," said D.J. "And I don't care."

Just then a light crossed Mom's face. D.J. dreaded that look. *One of her bright ideas, I suppose.*

"Why don't you invite Eddie to your birthday party?" she asked.

"Aw, Mom, you gotta be kidding! He'd wreck the whole thing."

"I don't think so," Dad said quietly. "Your mother might have something there."

"I can't believe what you're saying! I should invite the meanest kid I know?"

"Well, maybe so," Dad answered.

"But I'm supposed to have fun at my party!" D.J. exclaimed.

"It might turn out to be just that."

"Oh, Dad!"

"Why don't you think about it?" he asked.

"I'll think, all right. I can't think of anything that would be worse." D.J. pushed back his chair to leave the table.

"Just a minute, D.J.," Dad said. "Let's have devotions before you leave." He slid a box of Bible verses forward. "We'll each pick a verse tonight."

D.J. wanted to escape, but he slowly pulled out a card. *Oh no!* he thought as he read what it said. He hoped Mom and Dad would forget his turn, but they didn't.

D.J. had no choice but to read aloud. " 'If your enemy is hungry, feed him; if he is thirsty, give him something to drink. . . . Do not be overcome by evil, but overcome evil with good' " (Romans 12:20–21).

Mom and Dad laughed. D.J. didn't. "I said I'd think about it!" The anger rose in his voice. "What am I supposed to do?"

D.J. pushed the whole thing to the back of his mind until the next day. When he saw Eddie in the hall, he remembered what Mom and Dad had said. Yet every feeling within D.J. shouted *No!*

Once again he tried to avoid Eddie, but couldn't. As the bully edged up, D.J. stepped back.

In the next instant a thought came to him. *Why don't I invite Eddie and be really mean to him? I could do it so Mom and Dad wouldn't know. They'd stop pestering me, and I'd still win.*

For a moment D.J. thought about the idea. *What can I do to get even?*

A secret glee welled up inside him. D.J. straightened to his full height. He still came only to Eddie's shoulder, but his words sounded strong and sure. "Eddie, do you want to come to my birthday party on Saturday? We're gonna play broomball, and Mom's fixing lots of food."

Eddie's face had a strange look. "You want *me* to come?"

"Sure," D.J. said, not really meaning it. But before Saturday he should be able to think of the biggest chunk of meanness ever invented. "Two o'clock, okay? And bring a broom. We'll play on the rink across the street from my house."

For the first time D.J. dreaded his birthday party. He looked forward to getting even with Eddie but hated himself for what he was going to do.

D.J. and his friends were already on the ice when Eddie showed up. He stood at the edge of the rink, his stubby, sawed-off broom in his hand. He looked as if he didn't know what to do.

I'll pretend I don't see him, D.J. thought. *I'll treat him like he's crashing the party. Then I'll let him play, and we'll all gang up on him.*

For the next ten minutes, D.J. stuck to his plan, making sure he didn't glance in Eddie's direction. In a break between plays, he couldn't help but see the lost look on Eddie's face.

Is that how I look when Eddie is mean to me? For a moment D.J. felt a sliver of sympathy for the bully, but he quickly pushed it aside. *I hope he's wondering if it's all a trick.*

Two plays later D.J. decided it was time for Plan B. "Come here, Eddie," he called. "You can be on my team."

The players took their positions. D.J. moved out, his broom extended like a hockey stick. The ball shot toward him. His broom connected, and the ball slid into the net.

Time after time D.J. took control of the ball. It seemed he could do no wrong. The score for his team mounted.

But Eddie was having big trouble. Somehow his arms and legs moved in opposite directions. More than once he landed flat on the ice and everyone hooted. Often he looked embarrassed. As the bully picked himself up, he glanced at D.J., as though wondering what he thought.

He's clumsy, D.J. decided. *Is it possible Eddie has never played before? I'm surprised he keeps trying.*

A small cut above Eddie's eye was bleeding. A secret smugness filled D.J. *What will happen when we gang up on him? He's so awkward, he won't have a chance.*

Once more the ball shot out. Eddie raced after it. As he took a swing, he fell hard and slid into the net. The net collapsed around him.

The other boys roared with laughter, but a sudden feeling of shame broke through D.J.'s wish for revenge. One part of him said, *I want to get even.* The other part asked, *Should I help him? What will the other kids think?*

In the next moment D.J. made up his mind. *I'll probably hate myself for this.*

Moving forward, he offered his hand and helped Eddie up. The bully looked surprised.

Inside, D.J. felt just as surprised about what he had done. Then he felt good.

TO **TALK** ABOUT

▸ When someone treats you in a mean way, how does it make you feel? What do you want to do?

▸ D.J. found one way to "feed" his enemy and "give him something to drink." How did D.J. "overcome evil with good"?

▸ How do you think Eddie acted during the rest of the party? How do you suppose D.J. and Eddie acted toward each other the next time they met?

▸ Is there a kid in your life who acts mean the way Eddie did with D.J.? What are some ways you can show kindness to that bully?

▸ How did Jesus act toward mean people in His life? Big clue: He acted more than one way. Try to name them. See John 8:59; John 11:54; Luke 22:47–51; Luke 23:34.

▸ D.J. found it worked to respond to meanness with kindness. But what if a mean kid keeps on taking advantage of you? What are some other ways to handle your problem?

▸ Compare your ideas with the ones that follow:

1) Walk away from the bully. Ignore him and his buddies.

2) Try to work out your conflict. Talk about what's

----

wrong. Explain your side of the problem. If your disagreement comes up in school, you may have peer mediators to help you.

3) Take your stand. If a bully keeps picking on you, talk to your mom or dad or another adult about how to defend yourself.

4) Remember something important: **If you hate someone, that person has won.**

Do not be overcome by evil, but overcome evil with good.
Romans 12:21

Jesus, when kids are mean, I want to keep hating them. I have a hard time believing I could do what D.J. did. But help me, Jesus. I want to act the way you did to the people who were mean to you.

Two Choices

All afternoon the sand had been warm. Bright sunlight touched the Minnesota lake with a thousand sparkles. It had been fun meeting new friends at Bible camp, but tomorrow it would all end.

Now a haze covered the sun. Christy shivered. Her swimsuit was damp and her fingernails blue from the cold. She stood up to go change her clothes, then heard Ryan's shout. "Hey, Christy, want a boat ride?"

"Just a minute," she called. "I'll change into jeans and be right back."

Inside her cabin, Christy heard a muffled sound from a back room. She paused and heard the noise again. Was someone crying?

Christy followed the sound to the bedroom. There she found Mia lying face down, weeping into her pillow.

What should I do? Christy wondered. *Pretend I don't see her? Or ask what's wrong?*

She wanted to change quickly and go back to the fun. Yet Mia's sobs shook the bed.

For a moment Christy stood there, thinking what to do. She hated scenes. She had been part of too many of them at home. Besides, her friends were waiting. Inside Christy a tug-of-war began.

Just then Mia blew her nose. Christy stepped forward. "Hey, what's wrong? Can I help?"

As Mia looked up, her shoulders stopped shaking. Her red, swollen eyes forced Christy to think back. As though seeing herself on a movie screen, she remembered the times she had fallen asleep crying.

Still feeling torn, yet knowing she'd hate herself if she didn't stay, Christy sat down on the edge of the bed. From somewhere came the courage to ask, "Did you get bad news about your dad?"

Mia shook her head.

"Then, what's wrong?"

"Oh, Christy, I'm scared." Mia spoke between sniffs. "This week has been so perfect, I don't want to go home. It's terrible watching Daddy get sicker every day."

Her words ended in a sob, but she tried again. "I'm scared he's going to die. What would I do without him?"

Help! Christy thought. *Where can I find a counselor?* Ready to look for one, she stood up.

But Mia spoke quickly. "Don't leave. Please don't go."

Christy felt like a kitten stranded high in a tree. *What can I say?* Slowly Christy sat down again. *Oh, God, how can I help her?*

In the next moment, words came into Christy's mind, and they didn't seem her own. Christy stumbled over them, but the words came out. "Mia, if something happens to your dad, you'll still have a Father."

"Do you mean Daddy will live forever?"

"I mean you can still have a heavenly Father."

"You mean *God*? What difference would that make?"

"All the difference in the world. He won't save you from every bad thing that happens, but He promises to be with you."

Mia sat up. "How do you know He'd be with me?" Her voice sounded resentful, yet her gaze clung to Christy's. "Your daddy isn't dying."

"No, but my parents are divorced. Dad lives way across the country, and I only see him one month a year."

Christy stopped and made herself uncurl her tense fingers. Now *she* was the one who wanted to cry. "What happened to me is different from what's happening to you. But when Dad left—" Christy swallowed, then went on. "When it was really hard, I found out how much I need to hang on tight to Jesus."

"What do you mean, Christy—hang on tight to Jesus?"

"To know Him. To love Him. To know way down deep how much He loves me."

Mia still looked doubtful. "He really truly helps you?"

"As long as I let Him. As long as I keep coming to Him, asking for help."

Mia's eyes seemed to brighten just a little. "If that's true, how can I know Him the way you're talking about? *Really* know Him, I mean."

Wondering how to explain, Christy stared at Mia. Her eyes wide open, Christy prayed. *Now what do I say, Lord?*

Then Christy remembered the night before and Pastor

Paul's talk on John 3:16. "There's a verse that kind of sums it up," Christy said.

As she repeated the words, her voice grew stronger. " 'For God loved the world so much that he gave his only Son, so that everyone who believes in him may not die, but have eternal life' " (TEV).

"Isn't that what Pastor Paul talked about?" Mia asked. "He wanted to know if we believed that Jesus died for our sins. But it doesn't seem real to me."

Her blue eyes held a question. "I have a hard time believing God can take care of me, especially if Daddy dies. Is that a sin—that I don't trust God? That I don't believe He's big enough to take care of me?"

Mia was quiet now, thinking about it. "Maybe that's what keeps me from God. I *need* the love of Jesus so much, but I'm so scared about Daddy." Once again tears welled up in her eyes.

Christy wanted to be honest. "I'm not smart enough to answer all your questions. But Pastor Paul said something else. We can't always know if we'll be okay. But if we ask Jesus to forgive us, that's the first step in learning to trust Him."

Christy cleared her throat. "Mia, would you like Jesus to come into your life?"

As Mia thought about it, the minutes seemed to last forever. Then she nodded. "Tell me what to pray."

Sentence by sentence, Christy led her. When Mia looked up from praying, a light shone in her eyes. "Strange!" she said. "How can one prayer make so much difference? But down here it's real!" Mia tapped her chest. "God really does love me!"

In that moment Christy knew without a doubt that her words had not been her own. Reaching out, she hugged Mia.

Oh, Lord, you are wonderful! Christy thought. *What if I had sneaked out instead of talking to Mia? Oh, God, thank you!*

TO **TALK** ABOUT

▸ What choice did Christy make when she heard Mia crying?

▸ What choice did Mia make about her relationship with Jesus?

▸ Will all of Mia's problems instantly be over? How will Jesus help her deal with her problems?

▸ Do you need to say Christy's prayer for help in telling someone about Jesus? He promises to give you the words to say.

▸ Do you know for sure that Jesus is your Savior and Lord? **Coming to salvation in Jesus is the most important choice you will ever make.** If you would like to invite Him into your life, you can use your own words or offer Mia's prayer:

"Thank you, Jesus, for dying on the cross for me. I'm sorry for my sins and ask your forgiveness. I ask you to be my Savior. To be Lord over every part of my life—even the part of me that's scared. Thank you, Jesus, for your sal-

It is by the name of Jesus Christ of Nazareth. . . . Salvation is found in no one else, for there is no other name under heaven given to men by which we must be saved. Acts 4:10, 12

Everyone who calls on the name of the Lord will be saved. Romans 10:13

Thank you, Jesus, that when I ask your forgiveness, you do forgive all my sins. Thank you that through your death on the cross, you give me salvation and eternal life. Thank you for making it real to me. I want to hang on tight to you all the days of my life and forever.

If you have prayed, asking Jesus for His salvation, it's important that you talk to someone about it. If you do, your prayer and what you have received from Jesus will seem more real to you. Find out how you can keep growing in Jesus.

vation. For your eternal life beginning right now. Amen!"

SECRETS OF THE BEST CHOICE

Surfing the Web

When Jordan got home from school, the boxes were in the family room.

"Way to go!" he exclaimed. "You bought the computer today!"

Mom smiled. "When I got off work, I stopped by for it. But let's wait till your dad gets home so he can set it up."

In the past few weeks Mom and Dad had been shopping for a new computer. For a while they had wondered if they really wanted a home computer with the ability to connect with the Internet. They had talked about the giant network that connected people and information around the world.

"It would help Jordan with his homework, wouldn't it?" Mom had asked.

"If he's going to keep up with our world, he needs to be comfortable with the technology," Dad said.

For years Dad had used a computer at work. Not long ago Mom had also gone online. At first she came home from work exhausted because she needed to learn so much. "It's like being in a small box with the sides closing in on my brain," she said.

"Let's put the computer in my room," Jordan told Mom now. "If I use it for homework, that would be a good place." *And I can surf the Net any time I want*, he added to himself.

But Mom shook her head. "We'll keep the computer in the family room. That way we'll be right here if you need help."

Need help! Jordan thought of his computer classes at school. *I know more than you do, Mom!*

After their evening meal, Dad set up the computer and talked with Jordan about the screen name he would use instead of his own. When Jordan was out of the room, Dad chose the parental controls he wanted and entered the password. When Jordan returned, Dad explained that Jordan didn't need to know the password.

"But I want to know it!" Jordan said.

"If it's not in your head, you won't be tempted to use it the wrong way," Dad told him. "I've set the controls so you can access the kids' chat rooms, but you can't go into the adult ones."

A flash of resentment shot through Jordan. "So you don't trust me!"

"I trust you," Dad said. "But I don't trust everyone else. When you're using chat rooms, you can meet anyone in the world who decides to come online. That can be exciting. And with email, your mom will have a chance to talk to her sisters in Texas, Greece, and Kenya. But there are drawbacks, too. You might meet adults who pretend they're a kid."

"That's no big deal!" Jordan scoffed. "Wherever they are, they're at the end of the wire, not here in this room."

Dad shook his head. "It might seem that way, but you know better than to talk to a stranger you meet at the mall or in a park, don't you?"

Jordan nodded.

"Same deal. So if you're going to use the Internet, we need to agree on the rules."

Jordan sighed. *Rules, rules, rules! Everything I do has rules wrapped around it!*

"We want you to have a good experience," Dad went on. "When you're surfing the Net, if you click at the wrong place or type a wrong address, you can come up with some pretty weird stuff. That's why we're here to help."

When they logged on, Dad showed Jordan a kids' page. And sure enough, right in front of Jordan were more rules.

"Let's stop here," Dad said. "This will help you enjoy the Internet. Let's see if we agree on what it says."

As they talked about the rules, Dad explained the reasons for them. In spite of his wish to get surfing, Jordan had to admit it helped to understand why Dad and Mom wanted to give him safety tips.

"Sometimes people put things on the Internet that I don't want to see, even as an adult," Dad said. "I don't want that kind of thing in my mind. If I know a Web site has something like that, I refuse to open it."

Then Dad added some more ideas. "We know your neighborhood and school friends. We want to know your online friends, too. And just like we know the TV programs you watch, we'll visit Web sites with you. It'll be fun doing it together."

When they agreed upon the rules, Dad explained something else. "If you spend too much time online, we'll handle it like TV."

Jordan groaned, but Dad went on. "We'll set limits so you get out with your friends here in the neighborhood. You can't substitute a computer for real people."

As they visited Web sites, Jordan came to a place where kids could offer their ideas about a topic. Jordan clicked a subject called "My Hero."

He liked seeing what other kids wrote about sports heroes, famous people, and friends. Suddenly Jordan stopped scrolling and read an answer a second time. *Hmmm. I never thought about it that way!*

He made sure that both Mom and Dad read the message:

My heroes are my parents. They love me so much that they care about everything I do.

As Jordan went to bed that night, he was still thinking about the power of the Internet for good or evil. *It's no wonder Mom and Dad want to protect me. Maybe they know more than I give them credit for.*

To Jordan's surprise he had learned something even bigger than safety ideas for going online. *Sticking with the right rules gives me the freedom to travel around the world!*

TO **TALK** ABOUT

▶ What are some good ways to use the Internet? What are some negative things about the Internet?

▶ Do you think setting boundaries for surfing the Web is a good idea? Why or why not?

▶ Why do you think Jordan might not want his parents to know everything he sees or reads through email, chat rooms, and the Internet?

▶ Do Jordan's parents have the right to say what Jordan can do on the computer? Give ideas to back up your opinion.

▶ Do the risks of what you might see or hear apply only to the Internet? In what other areas do you need to be on guard? Why?

▶ **Though your mom and dad use parental controls, there's an even more important control—when your own brain and heart say no.** How can your ability to say no protect and help you? Give examples.

▶ What are your family's safety rules for the Internet? On the next page are some ideas that are important wherever you access the Internet—home, school, the library, or a friend's house.

Sample Family Internet Rules

1. I will not tell anyone on the Internet my full name, address, telephone number, or the name of my school without my parents' permission.
2. I will remember that some kids I meet in chat rooms may not really be kids. Sometimes bad people pretend to be kids in chat rooms.
3. I will not meet any of my online friends in person for the first time unless it is in a public place and my father or mother is with me.
4. I will treat others the way I want them to treat me. I will never send out mean messages nor will I respond with mean messages to any that are sent to me.
5. I will stop immediately if I come across anything that makes me feel uncomfortable. It is not my fault if I accidentally see something bad. If I do, I will get offline or turn off my computer. And I will tell my parents what happened.
6. I will not go online over ___ hours per week.
7. I will follow my family's guidelines for Net safety.

Signed _____

(Have all family members sign here.)

Date _____

Taken from: *Safety Net* Copyright © 1998 by Zachary Britton. Published by Harvest House Publishers, Eugene, Oregon 97402. Used by permission.

"Honor your father and your mother, so that you may live long in the land the Lord your God is giving you." Exodus 20:12

Lord, you know that often I get upset about rules. Help me remember that usually there's a good reason for them. Protect me, Jesus, in all that I do and see and take in. I want to hang on tight to you. I trust you to help me!

Home, Sweet Home

Through the school bus window, Annie gazed at the farms they passed. White houses shone in the autumn sun. Silos stood tall. Cows and horses grazed quietly.

Annie felt as if she were seeing them for the first time. She sneaked a look at Tricia, wondering how her friend from school would like her house and family.

I was crazy to invite her home, Annie thought as nervous jiggles bounced around her insides. *Whatever made me do it?*

As though she could hear Annie's thoughts, Tricia spoke. "I've always wanted to visit you."

Then Annie remembered how this had come about. Tricia had practically invited herself! Would she be disappointed in what she saw? Would she like Annie's older brother and sister, Josh and Sue? Even now they sat at the back of the bus with the older kids. And what would Tricia think of the room Annie shared with four-year-old Dawn?

Around Annie kids talked about what had happened at school that day. But Annie was quiet, thinking back to her visit to Tricia's. What a room she had! A canopy bed with a flouncy spread. Her own CD player and computer. Stuffed animals all over the room. And a beautiful, big, quiet house. No brothers or sisters to fight with or mess things up!

Brakes squealed, and the bus ground to a halt. Silently Annie began to pray. *I'm scared, Lord. I don't know if I can handle it if Tricia doesn't like our place. What if she even tells me so, the way she does when she doesn't like something at school? You take care of it, Jesus, will you?*

Out of long habit, Annie stood up, clutched her book bag, and followed Sue and Josh down the steps. Tricia trailed behind.

At least our driveway isn't muddy right now, Annie thought.

As always, her little sister, Dawn, stood at the door, waiting for Annie, Josh, and Sue to come home. Annie knelt down to give Dawn a hug. "Hi, kitten. This is my friend Tricia."

Tricia stopped to look into the little girl's face. "How old are you?" she asked.

Dawn held up four fingers. "Next year I go to school!" She tucked her hand into Annie's. "I made cookies for you today."

Annie grinned, knowing Dawn must have had quite a bit of help from Mom. The aroma of freshly baked cookies still lingered in the air. Annie walked into the kitchen and introduced Tricia just as Mom poured large glasses of milk.

Mom's smile was as warm as the kitchen. *So far, so good,* Annie thought as she and Tricia joined Sue and Josh at the table. But five minutes later Josh rolled his eyeballs toward heaven and smirked at Sue.

"Stop it!" she cried. Under the table her foot came down hard on Josh's toes.

He jumped up, shaking his foot as he limped around the kitchen. "Ow, ow, ow! You do too like him! Say that you do!"

"Joshua." Mom's voice held a warning.

Sue's face was red and her eyes bright with unshed tears. "Be quiet, Josh!" she muttered.

"I saw you looking at him. I saw you passing notes on the bus," he teased.

Sue stood up, set her glass down hard, and ran blindly to her room.

Annie wanted to crawl under her chair. Again she sneaked a look at her friend. Tricia had a quiet smile on her face. She seemed just plain interested. How could anyone be interested in watching a brother and sister fight?

Slowly Annie pushed back her chair. *Well, I guess I better get it over with. I wonder how Tricia will like my room.*

Moments later Tricia stood at the door. As she looked around, Annie watched her. Tricia's gaze stopped on the second bed.

"Dawn sleeps here, too?" she asked. "You get to talk at night whenever you want?"

Annie nodded. *What is Tricia thinking?* she wondered.

Then Annie started to giggle.

TO **TALK** ABOUT

▸ Why do you think Annie giggled? What clues tell you how Tricia felt about what she was seeing?

▸ What if Tricia hadn't liked Annie's room and family? What would Annie need to decide?

▸ Farm animals often stick their heads between barbed wire to munch the grass on the other side. They think it's better than the grass on their own side. How did Annie think the grass was greener on the other side of the fence? What did she see in Tricia's life that seemed better than her own life?

▸ How can you choose to like your own home, even though it's different from your friends' homes? What happens if you focus on the good things about your home and family?

▸ God wants families to offer love and a sense of caring for each other. What other qualities make us feel that a home is a good place to be?

▸ What matters most—the material things in a home or the love and support that family members give to each other? Why?

▸ **Loyalty in a family means sticking together, building each other up, and telling other people good things about your family.** (That kind of loyalty is different from talking to someone if a family member is hitting or hurting you in some way.) Why is it important to be loyal to your family? What are some ways you can show your loyalty?

▸ How can you pray for your family? What are some things you can ask God to do?

Keep me from paying attention to what is worthless; be good to me, as you have promised. Psalm 119:37 (TEV)

Jesus, when I compare what other kids have to what I don't have, that's paying attention to worthless things, isn't it? Even though my family isn't perfect, I thank you for giving it to me. Thank you that this is where I belong. Give me your big love for every person in my family.

A Look in the Mirror

Elise hated using the mirror in the school bathroom. The light gave her skin a funny color. Every spot and blemish showed. And today she felt even more critical of her appearance than usual.

Taking out her brush, she tried once more to bring her hair over the zits on her forehead. *No matter what I do, I can't hide them,* she thought.

Next she inspected her eyes. *I wish they were big and brown like my friend Rosa's. How can I ever be popular the way I look?*

Elise was so busy looking at herself that she barely noticed the girl who had come in. A strange movement in the mirror caught Elise's attention.

What's she doing? Elise wondered.

The girl wore a cute hat that fit close around her head. When she twisted it in place, Elise saw under the brim.

Did I imagine it? she asked herself. Then she knew she hadn't. The girl was bald!

Just then Elise realized she'd been caught staring. *Oh*

wow! Red crept into her face. *There I go again—forgetting how someone else might feel.*

Picking up her books, Elise turned to leave, but something clicked in her mind. *The girl with cancer. She just started two of my classes.*

Everyone had been talking about the girl and the chemotherapy she was taking. Some even said she'd lost all her hair. The rumor must be true.

Elise turned back in time to see a tear roll down the girl's cheek. Other tears followed. The silent weeping made Elise feel terrible. *Should I say something? Or pretend I don't notice?*

For a moment she stood there, trying to decide. The girl acted as if she didn't see her. At last Elise spoke. "I'm Elise. What's your name?"

The girl's lips quivered. "Yolanda. Yolanda Garcia." Leaning down, she turned on a faucet and splashed cold water on her face. "I'll be all right," she mumbled.

But Elise felt sure Yolanda was just trying to be brave. "I don't know what's wrong, but can I help?"

Yolanda turned to face her. "Help? I wish you could." If the words hadn't sounded so hopeless, Elise would have thought the girl was bitter. Instead, she seemed ready to give up.

"What's wrong?" Elise asked.

As Yolanda turned off the faucet, her tears started again. "I've never been so embarrassed in all my life. Both yesterday and today—" As if unable to stand up anymore, she braced herself against the sink.

Elise waited, feeling embarrassed herself. She didn't like being uncomfortable.

Yolanda drew a long, ragged breath. "Some mean boys found out—" She struggled to speak. "Some boys found out that I've lost my hair. When I walk through the hall, they come up behind me and pull off my hat."

"Oh no!" Elise said, but she held back her thoughts. *And I don't like my hair and the color of my eyes!*

Yolanda's shoulders shook with sobs, but no sound escaped. Elise stood there wondering what to do.

"I can't walk down that hall again," Yolanda finally said. "Taking chemo is bad enough. But I can't handle how the boys laugh when they see my bald head."

As the girl's pain pierced her heart, Elise began praying. *Oh, God, forgive me! Maybe Mom is right when she tells me to stop spending so much time at the mirror!*

Turning on the faucet, Yolanda again bent down to splash water on her face.

Elise wanted to run. Instead, she prayed with her eyes open. *Jesus, I don't know what to do. You're going to have to show me. Help!*

As Yolanda straightened up, she drew a deep breath and looked in the mirror. Once more she turned her hat and settled it on her head. When she tried to smile, her lips trembled. "Well, how do I look?"

"Great!" Elise said. But she hurt inside, just thinking how it would feel to have no hair. "Let's figure out what we can do."

"I've tried," Yolanda answered. "I need something to do.

I don't want to stay home all day. I want to be here with everyone else, but . . ."

But now Elise had an idea. "You said the boys come up behind you? Then I'm going to walk behind you!"

"You mean it?" Hope leaped into Yolanda's eyes. "You really mean it?"

"Yup." Elise sounded more confident than she felt. "I'll walk behind you whenever you go through the hall. I'll make sure none of the boys get near you."

Yolanda looked as if she wanted to believe her but wasn't sure she could.

Elise kept on. "You're in two of my classes, so I'll walk with you before and after. I'll talk to the other girls, and we'll work out a system for the rest of your classes."

Yolanda smiled, and it was like the sun coming out after a storm.

Elise laughed. "We'll fool those mean boys!"

Like a soldier going into battle, Yolanda straightened her shoulders. With Elise behind her, Yolanda walked into the hall.

TO **TALK** ABOUT

▸ How do you think Elise will feel about herself the next time she looks in the mirror? In what ways can you be thankful about your own appearance?

▸ There's a difference between showing pity and giving understanding. Showing pity means we act as if we're sorry for someone but wouldn't want to be like them. We offer sweet, kind-sounding words but no real help. What might have happened to Yolanda if Elise had treated her that way?

▸ Giving understanding means that we let someone know we feel sorry about what's happening to them, but we also offer support. In what way did Elise give understanding to Yolanda?

▸ Pity takes away whatever hope or self-confidence a hurting person has left. **Understanding helps a person go on, even though it's hard.**

▸ Why was it important to Yolanda that she keep going to school?

▸ Have there been times when you've made fun of someone because you didn't understand what was happening? If possible, how would you change that now?

▸ While Jesus lived on earth, He showed that He cared about people and what happened to them. How did He also help them in practical ways? Look for clues in Mark 6:30–44 and John 11:32–44.

"So do not fear, for I am with you; do not be dismayed, for I am your God. I will strengthen you and help you; I will uphold you with my righteous right hand." Isaiah 41:10

Jesus, it's so easy to be selfish and think only about myself. I choose to care about the hurts and needs of people around me. Help me to love them with your love and find practical ways to help.

If You Tell
I'll...

"C'mon, Scott." Mitch took off down the hall, walking so fast Scott could barely keep up with him.

"Where you going?" Scott asked.

"There's not much time. I'll show you."

Scott dropped his books into his locker and followed his friend. Soon they were outside, and the brisk wind felt good after being in school all day. But Scott still wanted to know where they were going. He asked again.

"I'm meeting some kids at a house down the street," Mitch told him. "Have to be there in five minutes. They'll leave if I'm not on time. *C'mon!*"

The urgency in his voice sparked Scott's interest. Mitch took off, his long legs covering the distance in great leaps.

A block later Mitch slowed his pace, looked up and down the street, and turned onto a narrow path between trees. By the time they reached the house, Scott was out of breath and struggled to speak. "What's going on? Who lives here?"

"Never mind. You're my friend, and I want you with me." Mitch knocked on a side door.

In one split second, the door opened as if by magic. Scott could see no one, but Mitch stepped inside. As Scott held back, Mitch reached out and tugged at his sleeve.

"Come on," Mitch said sharply. *"Move!"*

As soon as Scott was inside, Mitch closed the door. Scott stood next to it while his eyes adjusted to the change of light. In the dim kitchen, he saw Mitch reach out for a small packet. A moment later it disappeared. Then Scott and Mitch were outside again.

As Mitch reached the street, he looked both ways, up and down the sidewalk, then started back to school.

"Now will you tell me what that was all about?" demanded Scott.

"Sure, you're in on it now. Got some for you to try."

"Got some what for me to try?" Slowly light dawned on Scott, and he stopped dead still in the middle of the sidewalk.

"Mitch, what do you mean?" The full understanding of what they had just done staggered Scott. "Do you mean drugs? You're doing drugs? But we agreed! We promised each other!"

"We promised each other we'd always do things together. That's what being friends is, isn't it? So I brought you along. I want you to give it a try."

But Scott was angry now. "That promise did not mean we should do something wrong together. Doing drugs will hurt us!"

"You sure about that, little boy? Is that what your parents say? How do you know if you haven't tried it? I want to find out for myself."

"I don't wanna listen to you," Scott snapped. "You're thinking crazy! Have you already tried some?"

"Well . . ." Mitch didn't meet his eyes.

"Well, I'm not with you on this one," Scott said.

"Aw, c'mon," answered Mitch. "You can't do that to me. We're friends. I let you in on something good."

"Something bad, you mean." Scott felt as if he couldn't say it strongly enough. "I'm not part of this one!"

"Oh yes, you are! You went to the house. If I get caught, I'll tell people you took me there."

Scott's stomach bottomed out. He *was* part of it. He had stood there watching Mitch take the packet and hadn't said a word.

What can I do? Scott felt desperate now.

"And don't you dare tell on me," Mitch said. "If you squeal, I'll beat you up!"

"Beat up on me?" Scott felt scared now, as if a million motorcycles circled a track in his brain. They seemed to make so much noise that he couldn't think straight.

I hate it when kids squeal on others, when they go running like a baby to their mama. But is this the same? Not tell anyone? Not even Mom or Dad? What if Mitch gets hooked?

In that moment the motorcycles stopped. Scott's head cleared. *If Mitch gets hooked, would it be my fault because I didn't say anything?*

But now Mitch leaned over, towering above him. "If you tell on me, I'll get a whole bunch of guys to beat up on you! I mean it! Promise you won't say a word!"

Inside Scott the motorcycles started again. Again he felt

mixed up, and his tongue wouldn't move. Then the words came. "I promise—"

He stopped. "No, I don't."

For an instant Scott stood there. Then he ducked out of Mitch's reach. Knowing they would probably never be friends again, Scott started for home at a run.

TO **TALK** ABOUT

▸ What do you feel Scott should do—tell his parents about Mitch and what he's doing, or keep quiet? Give reasons for your answer.

▸ What does it mean when a kid tattles, or tells on someone? Compare that with what it means to tell a responsible person about something that may hurt people. Why is it important to talk with a responsible grown-up?

▸ If Scott keeps saying no to drugs, what will happen to his friendship with Mitch? Is a friendship worth keeping at any cost? If Scott tries to keep his friendship with Mitch, what might happen to Scott's life?

▸ In what ways have you needed to say no to what friends wanted you to do? Has that affected your friendship with them? Think about this: **A friend who is really a friend won't ask you to do something that hurts you.**

▸ When Jesus left His disciples here on earth, He promised to send the Holy Spirit to give them the power they needed to witness and live their daily lives. **Jesus wants** to give that same kind of power to you. The more empty and helpless you are, the more power you are able to receive.

▸ Being a Christian comes first. (See "Two Choices," p. 91.) If you are a Christian, ask Jesus to clean up every part of your life. Then ask Him for His gift of power: *Jesus, in your name I ask you to fill me with all the power of your Holy Spirit. Thank you!*

"But you will receive power when the Holy Spirit comes on you; and you will be my witnesses in Jerusalem, and in all Judea and Samaria, and to the ends of the earth." Acts 1:8

Help me, Jesus, to run away from doing wrong things. In your name I ask for all the power of your Holy Spirit. Help me to say such a strong NO! that kids know I mean it and leave me alone. Give me courage, too, so that someone's life isn't harmed because I'm afraid to speak to the right person at the right time. Thank you, Jesus, for your Holy Spirit power.

Gift From a Grandma

Skates flashed in the afternoon sun. Her long blond ponytail flying out, Karin spun like a top. As she twirled to a stop, her friends from school clapped.

Eric's eyes shone in admiration. "You did it, Karin! Way to go!"

"You didn't even wobble," said her best friend Amy.

Karin felt the warm flush of being praised spread across her cheeks. It felt good to do something well, and the crisp afternoon air gave the day a special brightness. Around her, the pond was filled with skaters, some sure of themselves, others still wobbly. Karin wished the day could last forever.

"Hey, you know what would be fun?" asked Amy. "Let's have a skating party tomorrow night."

"Sounds great!" Eric said. "It's the only night this week they'll have the lights on."

Happiness welled up inside Karin. "That's a good idea, Amy. You and I can ask the girls, and, Eric, why don't you ask the boys, and— Oh no!"

"What's the matter?" Eric asked.

"The kids at church are going to a nursing home tomorrow night. We're supposed to sing Christmas carols and talk to people."

"Oh, Karin!" Amy made a face. "Can't you skip it? It would be so much more fun to be here."

"I know." Karin thought about being cooped up inside stuffy halls. Then she thought about how much she liked to skate. Besides, Eric would be here, and of all the boys at school, he was the nicest.

"No one will ever know if you skip the singing," said Amy.

"Maybe you're right," Karin answered. "But what if everyone thinks the same thing? What if no one shows up?"

She looked at Eric, hoping that he, too, would tell her to skip the singing, but he didn't. Instead, he asked, "Can you do both? Come here after the nursing home?"

Karin shook her head. "It's way downtown." But her thoughts raced on. *If I could figure out a way to get out of singing . . .*

Suddenly Karin made a quick turn on the ice. *I promised I'd be there. The church kids set the time for when I could come.*

As she scraped to a halt, Karin knew she was only trying to fool herself. "You have the party anyway," she said to her friends. Karin knew her words were right, but inside she felt awful.

The next evening Karin still felt disappointed about not being with her friends. Going up the steps of the nursing home, she couldn't help but think of the skating party. Yet she looked around the small caroling group and knew she was needed.

Warm air greeted them as they started down the hall. "Joy to the world! The Lord is come. . . ." Karin sang as loud as she could but wondered what Eric and Amy and the others were doing.

A heavily decorated tree stood in the middle of the large room they entered. Its soft lights cast a glow on the elderly people gathered around. "Away in a manger, no crib for his bed, the little Lord Jesus lay down his sweet head. . . ."

In that moment all thoughts of the skating party vanished, for Karin caught sight of a little white-haired lady sitting in a wheelchair. Dressed in her Sunday best, she sat with her hands folded in her lap. Her gaze clung to the faces of the singers. Quietly, as though she didn't know what was happening, a tear started down her cheek.

When they finished singing, Karin went to her. "I'm Karin," she said. "You remind me of my great-grandma Lydia, who died last year."

"And you look like my granddaughter who lives far away," said the little lady. "Call me Grandma Dee if you like." Her smile was like the sun coming out from beneath a cloud.

Soon it was time for Karin to go. Grandma Dee reached forward to tuck something into her hand. "Thank you," she said. "You brought Christmas to me."

Looking down, Karin saw a white handkerchief with beautiful lace around the edge. She knew the little woman had used it to dry her tears.

Grandma Dee smiled again. "I love you," she said.

Now it was Karin's turn to blink away tears. "I love *you*," she answered, as if she were talking to her great-grandma. Leaning forward, she put her arms around the little woman.

As Karin gave her a quick hug, she felt surprised at how much her new friend meant to her. Then she turned and hurried with the others to the van.

For the first time since entering the building, Karin remembered the skating party. Yet she didn't feel sorry. She knew she had made the right choice.

Quietly Karin started humming a Christmas carol. *Should I go back to see Grandma Dee again?* she asked herself. *I think I know.*

TO **TALK** ABOUT

▸ Why was Karin's choice especially hard to make? What are some hard choices you've needed to make?

▸ If Eric is as nice as Karin thinks, how do you suppose he felt about Karin's choice to go to the nursing home? Why was it important that she kept her promise?

▸ Why do visitors mean so much to people in a nursing home? What did Karin receive that was better than a handkerchief?

▸ **A person who keeps promises is someone other people can trust.** Would you like to be known as someone who keeps promises? Why? What are some important promises you've made and kept?

▸ Once in a while, a person may promise to do something with you and then not be able to do it because of illness or another good reason. If that happens to you, how can you help the person who truly wanted to keep the promise?

"Give, and it will be given unto you. . . . For with the measure you use, it will be measured to you." Luke 6:38

Show me, Lord, how you want me to give to others. Help me plan my time so I can have fun with my friends but also keep the promises I make. Give me your love for the people you want me to help. Thank you for the way you love me.

Getting Even

As soon as they finished eating lunch, Marcos and his friends spilled out of the school onto the playground. To Marcos this was the best time all day, second only to gym class.

In a few minutes the kids had chosen sides for softball. Marcos took his usual place as shortstop. The softball game was well under way when Willy came to bat.

With three balls and two strikes against him, Willy hit a line drive between the pitcher's mound and third base. Marcos snagged the ball and threw it to first base. Seconds after the ball thudded into the baseman's mitt, Willy ran across first.

"You're out!" cried the first baseman, Jon.

Willy turned on him. "Out? You're crazy!"

Jon stood up to him. "You know I'm right!"

"Hey, stupid! You are wrong!"

"You are *out!*" Jon said again.

"No way! I made it by a mile!" Willy clenched his fist.

Uh-oh! Marcos broke into a run for first base. But he was too late. Willy's fist shot out in a strong right to Jon's stomach. Jon dropped to the ground, doubled over in pain.

"Hey, c'mon, Willy, knock it off!" Marcos said.

By now the rest of the team had gathered around. But Willy paid no attention to them. As though blinded by anger, he charged forward like an angry bull. Heading straight for where Jon lay on the ground, he drew back his leg for a kick.

Marcos grabbed Willy's shoulder and yanked him away. Just then the playground aide broke in. "What's going on here?"

When she understood what had happened, she said, "Willy, you're out of the game for the rest of the week."

His eyes filled with hate, Willy glared at her.

But the aide did not back down. "Tomorrow go to the detention room during lunch hour."

Willy kicked at the ground as though saying, "That's what I think about that!"

"And I'll talk to your teacher about your lack of respect," the aide went on.

Just then the bell rang. Kids headed back to the building. As they lined up outside the door, Marcos stood behind Willy and one of his buddies. Just watching Willy, Marcos could feel his anger—an anger so deep that Willy seemed ready to explode.

"You sure packed a good punch," his friend told him. "That was as good as TV."

Long ago Marcos had learned that Willy and his buddies had a favorite show—a show Marcos wasn't allowed to see.

Now Willy smirked. "Did you watch last night? Did you see that guy?" Clenching his fists, Willy jabbed the air. *"Pow, pow, pow!"*

His eyes filled with anger again. "If that aide hadn't stopped me, I could have cleaned up on Jon. Just wait. Tomorrow morning I'll get even at the bus stop."

"You will?" the friend asked eagerly.

"I've got it all figured out," Willy said. "I'll teach that stupid Jon a thing or two. He won't get *me* in trouble again. Wanna help?"

"What are you gonna do?"

Willy glanced around. His gaze rested on Marcos. Quickly Marcos turned away as though he hadn't heard Willy's threats. Then the line moved forward, and kids passed into the school.

But Marcos still felt the cold chill that slid down his spine.

TO **TALK** ABOUT

▸ **Words are very powerful. Some words hurt.** When someone says, "You're stupid," or "No one likes you anyway," feelings are hurt. What hurtful words did Willy use with Jon? What happened to the softball game because Willy used hurtful words?

▸ Some words are threats. Words such as "I'm going to get even" or "I'm going to kill that person" aren't a joke. It's the same as joking about blowing up a school. Certain words are seen as threats and will be taken seriously by teachers, principals, and other responsible people.

▸ **Good words and bad words have consequences.** If people use good words, there are usually good consequences. If people use hurtful or threatening words, there are often bad consequences. As the children lined up to go into school, Willy used words that are threats. Use your imagination to decide what choice each boy will make:

Willy: What is he going to do about his threat to get

even with Jon? Will he carry it out? Give reasons for your answer.

Willy's friend: Will he help Willy get even with Jon? If so, what do you think will happen?

Marcos: Will he pretend he doesn't know what's going on? Or will he talk to a responsible person about Willy's threat? Why is that different from running to a teacher to tell on a kid about something that isn't important? What if Marcos doesn't talk to a responsible person and something bad happens?

▸ Sometimes kids read about violent behavior or see it through TV, videos, or movies. If kids take in a lot of mean, negative behavior, they might not be clear in their thinking about what is real and what is just a story. Like Willy, they may act out negative behavior on the playground. How does that make you feel about what you want to put into your own mind? Explain.

▸ Describe how hurtful or threatening words make you feel. Describe how good words make you feel.

▸ What kind of words do you want to use? Why? Give examples of what you want to say to others.

I have set the Lord always before me. Because he is at my right hand, I will not be shaken. Psalm 16:8

Jesus, I don't want to run scared about everything I see and hear. But I do want to remember the importance of words. If there's a time when I need to talk with a responsible person, show me that. In good times and in hard choices, help me know what I should do. Then help me do it! And, Jesus, help me to use good words. Thanks!

Thirty Minutes and Counting

Rosita twisted her flute together and set her music rack next to the open window. As she looked outside, a gentle breeze lifted the pages of her exercise book.

Down the street the kids had a volleyball game going. Through the warm summer air, the sounds came clearly. Rosita wished she were there.

"Mommmm!" she called. "Do I have to practice?"

Mom poked her head in the door. "Put in your half hour, and you'll be free the rest of the day."

Rosita glanced at the clock and sighed, making sure Mom heard her. "Why did I say I wanted to play the flute?" Rosita asked. "I must have had rocks in my head."

"No, you didn't," Mom answered. "Remember how much you liked hearing that flutist at church?"

"But I didn't know it was going to be so hard."

"We bought the flute," Mom said. "Give it a fair chance. See how you feel at the end of six months."

She started to leave, then turned. "I'm going to the store in a few minutes. I'll be back in less than an hour."

Mom disappeared, and once again Rosita faced her exercise book. " 'A note followed by a dot has its value increased one half,' " she read. "Phooey!"

Tapping her foot to keep time, she began playing. One, two, three, rest. One, two, three, rest.

Rosita stopped. The volleyball had rolled this way. As she watched, her friend Audrey ran to pick it up, then went back to the game.

Next Rosita tried her scales—G, A, B, C.

She paused. *How do I go from C to D?* Taking out the sheet of fingerings, Rosita stared at the circles her instructor had drawn on a paper.

Just then she heard her mom's car leave the garage. As quickly as she could, Rosita twisted her flute apart, put the instrument in its case, and hurried outside.

Moments later she was playing volleyball with her friends. When she felt uneasy, Rosita pushed it aside. *Mom will never know.*

All through the month of June, Rosita practiced with her music rack next to the window. She longed to be out with the kids. Always she looked forward to that moment when she would finish her thirty minutes.

Then one July morning something inside Rosita changed. After hurrying through the scales, she opened her book of songs. As she played the notes, her mind began thinking the words. "Jingle bells, jingle bells, jingle all the way. . . ."

The tune was catchy, and she played it several times, surprised that it sounded better with each try.

Next, Rosita found a song she had sung in her music class at school. Soon her lower lip was sore, and she felt lightheaded from blowing. But when she glanced at the clock, she discovered twenty-five minutes had passed.

That day Rosita moved her music rack away from the window. Somehow it didn't seem as important to watch the kids down the street.

The next Sunday morning the flutist was back in church. As she soared to the high notes, Rosita held her breath. *How does she do it?*

By now Rosita knew how hard it was to reach those notes. With her whole heart, she longed to play really well.

Will you help me, God? she whispered during the prayer that followed. *Will you help me play like that?*

Near the end of the service, the flutist swung into a quiet, simple melody. Rosita knew the words. "In my life, Lord, be glorified, be glorified. . . ." She wanted the clear high notes to last forever.

The next morning the melody was still in Rosita's mind. *I wish I could play it,* she thought. When she searched in her books, she couldn't find the song.

As soon as Rosita finished her scales, she started her other music. But the song from church kept coming back. "In my life, Lord . . ." As clearly as if she had just heard it, Rosita remembered the tune.

For the first time she began going up and down the scale, listening for the note she needed.

There it is! she thought when she finally stumbled across it. *It's E!* She tried again and found the second note. Now she felt excited. E, G, E, G. As she kept listening, she picked out the rest of the tune. Afraid that she would forget the notes, she played them again and again.

Just then Rosita glanced at the clock. She had gone five minutes over!

It struck her so funny that she laughed out loud.

TO **TALK** ABOUT

▸ When Rosita found it hard to practice, what poor choice did she make? How do you think Rosita would have felt about herself if she had given up when she found it hard to practice? Why?

▸ For most people, learning to play an instrument is hard work until they reach a breakthrough. What good choices helped Rosita come to the breakthrough where she liked playing the flute?

▸ Often we think of a reward as some good, outward thing that happens to us. **A reward can also come in the satisfaction we feel about what we've done.** How did Rosita receive a reward in both ways?

▸ If we ask God to help us learn to play an instrument, does that mean we don't have to practice? How do you know?

▸ What are some skills you've worked hard to learn? Describe what it was like to learn those skills, whatever they are. How do the new things you've learned help you stretch out and do even more?

Surely you will reward each person according to what he has done. Psalm 62:12

Jesus, you know I often find it hard to practice. Yet I believe you want me to keep trying. Thank you for the way you help me learn. Thank you for the abilities you have given me. I choose to use them to honor you.

I'm Scared, God

From the room below came the sound of voices. All his life Jeremy had gone to bed hearing the low murmur. Yet these last weeks and months the voices had a different sound.

Quickly Jeremy slipped out of bed and crept to the open stairway. Crouching on the wide floorboards of the old farmhouse, he peered down between the posts of the railing. His parents sat at the dining room table—Mom mending a pair of jeans and Dad bending over a pile of papers.

As Jeremy watched, his father ran his fingers through his hair. "I just don't know what to do. We've always tithed from our income, and we've kept our expenses as low as we can. But we've never had a year like this."

Because of long, heavy rains and flooding of their fields, Dad had needed to replant that spring. Jeremy knew the seed had cost his father big money. Then hail took the second crop.

Jeremy's mom reached out. "I'll try to get more hours at work. During winter, maybe you can get a job outside the farm."

But Dad shook his head. "No matter how I figure the

numbers, I can't meet the payment."

As if she heard the discouragement in his voice, Mom stood up and circled the table. Leaning down, she hugged him. "I know, Jim. I know. We've talked about it so often."

Dad pushed back the papers. "I feel like a failure. I'm working harder than I've ever worked, and it isn't enough." His voice rose. "I'm afraid we'll lose the farm."

Lose the farm? Jeremy wondered if he was hearing things. In his worst nightmares, he had never come up with something that awful.

"Shhh!" Gently Mom put her fingers across Dad's lips. "I don't want the children to hear."

Dad sighed. "If we lose the farm, they'll have to know."

"I don't blame you for being upset. I'm discouraged, too. And afraid. But at least we don't have a new house or new machinery to pay for. We've done everything we can to be careful."

As Jeremy watched, tears came into his mother's eyes. This time it was Dad's turn to give a hug, and his voice changed. "I keep thinking of what Jesus said about the sparrows and the lilies."

From memory Mom spoke softly. " 'Look at the birds of the air; they do not sow or reap or store away in barns, and yet your heavenly Father feeds them.' "

She paused, as though forcing herself to go on. " 'If that is how God clothes the grass of the field, which is here today and tomorrow is thrown into the fire, will he not much more clothe you, O you of little faith?' "

Mom's voice grew softer. " 'O you of little faith?' I never thought about it that way before. Jesus expects us to trust

Him—to believe He'll take care of us." Her voice broke, but she went on. "No matter what happens, we'll be together."

Without making a sound, Jeremy crept back to his room. For a long time he stood at the window, looking out under the light of the full moon. Nearby, from the branch of a large oak, hung the swing he'd used for as long as he could remember. Now he felt too old for it, but he wondered, *Will my little sister and brother grow up here, enjoying that swing?*

Farther away, the brown stubs of corn stalks stretched out across a field. Seeing them, Jeremy remembered the first time he drove the tractor—the planting, the growing, the harvest. Dad tossing a golden ear of corn to see if he would catch it. Was that all over now?

In that moment Jeremy realized how much the land meant to him. Land on which his family had lived for over one hundred years. *Did Grandpa and Great-Grandpa ever wonder if they'd lose the farm? Did they ever feel this way inside?*

A worry knot formed and tightened in Jeremy's chest. Returning to bed, he slid down beneath the quilt. "I'm scared, God," he began. "What if we. . . ?"

Then he remembered the verses he'd heard Mom and Dad talking about. Jeremy started his prayer over. "I'm scared, God, but you said you'd take care of every little bird. How can I stop worrying? How do I trust in you instead of being scared? Will you help me believe you're going to take care of us?"

TO **TALK** ABOUT

▸ Do you think Jeremy's family will lose the farm? If they're forced to leave the place they love, does that mean God didn't keep His promise to provide for them?

▸ Jeremy's dad mentioned tithing. What *is* tithing? Why is that an important part of whether our money stretches far enough for what we really need? For clues see Malachi 3:10–12.

▸ Does God take away all our problems just because we are Christians? Or is God with us in the midst of our problems? How do you know?

▸ What are some *good* things we might learn when our family faces a smaller income?

▸ Sometimes it's important to ask, "What if?" It helps us dream big dreams and look ahead. Other times asking "What if?" means we're afraid. Do you have a "What if?" that makes you afraid? If so, what can you do about it?

▸ How did Jeremy hang on tight to Jesus? Do you know other verses Jeremy could repeat to himself when he's afraid about the future? **How can *you* hang on tight to Jesus?**

"Seek first his kingdom and his righteousness, and all these things will be given to you as well. Therefore do not worry about tomorrow, for tomorrow will worry about itself." Matthew 6:33–34

Jesus, when I'm scared, I let all the things that bother me go round and round in my head. Yet you know what I need. Help me believe in your promises. Teach me to pray about things that worry me. If you take care of every little bird, you can take care of me. Thank you!

Lying to Myself

It took only a moment, and it was done. "I want to come home later tonight," said Jackie. "I'd like to go to Debbie's after school."

Mom looked her straight in the eyes. "You'll be at Debbie's? And you'll be home by 5:30?"

For a split second Jackie thought about her answer. Yet when she told the lie, it seemed easy. "Sure, Mom, at Debbie's. I'll be home at 5:30. Just in time for supper."

Avoiding Mom's eyes, Jackie gave her a hug, and a moment later she was out the door. As the below-freezing air hit her face, her cheeks began to tingle. Squinting her eyes against the blinding white snow, Jackie started the four long blocks to school.

Halfway there she met Margrit. "Can you come after school, Jackie?" she asked. "The boys said they could."

"Sure, I'll see you then. Mom didn't catch on. I told her I'm going to Debbie's."

Hours later, Jackie reached Margrit's front door. Bart and Fitz were already there, and a strong bass thumped from the

CD player. For a moment Jackie felt a twinge of uneasiness. More than once her mom had said, *"You can't go to Margrit's after school. I don't want you there, especially when her mother is at work."*

"Yeah, Mom, yeah," Jackie had promised just as often. Now she pushed down her uneasiness. *Mom will never find out,* she told herself. *I know how to handle older boys. I can take care of myself.*

Turning on her brightest smile, Jackie entered the living room. Over in the corner Bart stood up. "Hi, Jackie."

The way he said her name made Jackie uncomfortable, but she tried to ignore the feeling. Soon she slipped into the beat of the music and forgot the whispers of her conscience. *Sure is more fun dancing with Bart than being at Debbie's.*

But Bart kept moving closer. Each time Jackie stepped back, he followed. *I should like this,* Jackie thought. Instead, she felt pushed into a corner. Her uneasy feelings clutched at her stomach.

Just then the music stopped. "I found four glasses," Margrit said. "Let's break out my mom's wine."

"She'll notice," said Jackie, afraid to say no.

"No, she won't. Here's a bottle that's half empty. She won't catch on if we take some."

In that instant the tightness in Jackie's stomach turned to cold fear. But somehow the glass was in her hand.

"Drink up, Jackie," Bart said a few minutes later. "We're waiting for you."

Jackie took a big gulp and choked. As the drink went down her throat, it burned.

"Take more," said Bart. "The more you drink, the better it tastes."

Jackie set down her glass, unwilling to try another sip. She didn't like the way she had started to feel.

But Bart wanted to dance again. "C'mon," he demanded.

As Jackie stood up, she didn't feel like herself. She hated the feeling, but Bart's sweaty hands took hers. His grip tightened, and Jackie wanted to scream. *Mom was right. I can't handle this!*

Desperate now, Jackie glanced at her watch. Ten minutes after five. Suddenly she knew what to do.

"I said I'd be home at 5:30. Gotta go." Before anyone could answer, she picked up her coat and hurried out the door.

Whew! I'll never try that again! Jackie felt grateful for the two blocks she had to walk in the cold fresh air. But Mom was waiting at the door.

"Where have you been, Jackie?"

"I told you this morning where I was going," she answered. "Don't you remember I said I was going to Debbie's?"

Mom's gaze held steady. "I called, and you weren't there. Too bad you missed your cousins. The furnace at their school broke down, so they had a day off. Your aunt Laura drove them over. They thought it'd be fun to see you."

In that moment Jackie felt like throwing up. Okay, so Mom had learned the truth. Jackie knew she was in for it now. But she felt relieved, too. All the hiding, the awful feelings, the wine, the lies—all the telling herself it was okay when it wasn't. And she missed her favorite cousins besides!

Who am I lying to? Jackie asked herself. *To my mom or to myself?*

TO **TALK** ABOUT

▶ What did Jackie mean when she asked, *Am I lying to my mom or to myself?*

▶ How does one lie lead to another? How did Jackie's choices keep getting her into deeper trouble? What were the bad consequences of her lies?

▶ What are some reasons why a kid tries to hide what he or she is doing? Because Jackie lied, she had no safeguards to help her out. What are some dangers for *anyone* who tries to hide what he or she is doing?

▶ What are some of the dangers of hanging out with older kids?

▶ Parents are people who want you to use their help when it's needed. How can it help you to say, "My mom (or dad) said I have to be home at a certain time"? Or "My parents said I can't do that"?

▶ If your parents know that you're going to a party at someone's house, it's easy for them to make one phone call. Your mom or dad can ask another parent, "I understand there's going to be a group of kids at your house. Will you be home?" That parent will be glad your mom or dad called and respect your family for caring about you.

How can you work together as a family to make life easier for all of you? Make a list of practical ideas. Here's a starter that would have helped Dusti at her slumber party (see "Popcorn Plus," p. 21):

1. At any time of the day or night, it's okay to call Mom or Dad and ask for a ride home.

Do not let kindness and truth leave you. . . . Write them on the tablet of your heart. So you will find favor and good repute in the sight of God and man. Proverbs 3:3–4 (NASB)

Jesus, when I'm tempted to lie, give me the power of your Holy Spirit to be truthful. Help me so my words and actions are honest before you and before other people. Thank you that when I'm honest I can respect myself and hang on tight to you.

You Wanna Be a *What*?

Tim pushed his books to one side of his desk as Mrs. Irving stood to introduce the day's speaker. Each week the teacher had invited someone to talk about a career possibility. "Today it's our pleasure to have with us Dr. Kent Alvarez," she said.

The class clapped politely, but Tim leaned forward, not wanting to miss a word.

"Thanks for inviting me," Dr. Alvarez began. "I want to tell you why I decided to become a doctor."

As Tim listened, he felt as if he was hearing a dream come true. Everything Dr. Alvarez talked about sounded exactly like what Tim wanted to do—except for one thing. Tim wanted to be a doctor somewhere in Africa.

Soon Dr. Alvarez finished speaking and left. Tim's teacher cleared her throat. "I've been reading the papers you wrote about what you'd like to be. Tim, your paper is so good. I want everyone to hear it. You've expressed your thoughts well and understand how people feel."

As she began reading, Tim felt sweat gather on his back.

I understand how people think, all right. Now it will start all over again—the teasing, the name-calling. Tim wished he could disappear.

Instead, he caught the wink of Bryce, the boy across the aisle. Trying to ignore him, Tim looked down at his hands.

But Bryce soon passed him a note: *Help me, Doc! I scratched my elbow.*

Tim stared straight ahead. *Why can't Mrs. Irving tell them I'm a good ballplayer?*

The teacher kept reading: " 'I would like to use my training as a doctor to become a missionary. . . .' "

Just then Josie, the girl in front of Tim, turned around, smiled shyly, and turned back. The rustling in the room grew quiet. Now everyone listened. Tim felt sure that most of them were collecting more ways to make fun of him.

Finally Mrs. Irving finished. "Pssst," whispered Bryce.

Tim pretended not to hear.

"Hey, preacher man," Bryce said in a louder whisper. This time those around him turned to listen. "How can I get to Heaven?"

Two boys snickered. *All I want to do is get out of here*, thought Tim. *I'll never write another paper telling what I* really *think.*

At last the day ended, and Tim escaped outside. Questions flew at him like missiles.

"Why do you want to go to a place like that?" asked one girl. "It's much more fun around here."

A boy joined in. "Sure, be a doctor in the United States. But a *missionary*! You can't make big bucks as a missionary!"

As soon as he could, Tim left the others behind and headed home. *Am I the only one who wants to do something with my life?*

Faster and faster Tim walked, and his thoughts kept up with his steps. *Why doesn't something count unless I make lots of money doing it? Do I* really *want to help people by being a missionary doctor? Are the kids right, Lord?*

In the midst of the sidewalk Tim stopped, knowing the answer to his question would change his life.

It took only a moment for another question to flash through his mind. *Or do I know something the other kids don't know?*

As the weight of his decision fell away, Tim felt peaceful. A grin spread across his face.

TO **TALK** ABOUT

▸ When kids tease, does it always mean they don't like the person they make fun of? Why do kids sometimes tease a person they secretly respect?

▸ Would the others tease Tim less if he thought of a funny way to answer them? What could he say?

▸ Tim wonders if he's the only one who wants to do something with his life. Do you think that's true? What clue hints at what Josie believes?

▸ It's important for each of us to know the way in which God calls us. Why do you think Tim should keep his goal of becoming a missionary doctor?

▸ **Values are the principles, standards, and qualities we believe are important in life. The values we think are worthwhile give us a sense of purpose and help us decide how we want to live.** What do you think about choosing a career *only* on the basis of how much money you would make? Why do you feel that way? How would you answer Tim's final question?

▸ It's fun to do something worthwhile. It's fun to be a person who helps others. What gives you a sense of purpose in life?

Am I now trying to win the approval of men, or of God? Or am I trying to please men? If I were still trying to please men, I would not be a servant of Christ. Galatians 1:10

Jesus, forgive me when I care so much about being liked that I'm not the person you want me to be. Help me to be a friend to others, but to always keep my eyes on you. When I feel afraid and alone, show me the goals you want me to have. Whatever career I enter, I want to serve you. Help me get ready through the things I learn now.

Run to Win

For the third time Nat checked her shoelaces to be sure they were tightly tied. As she went through her warm-up exercises, the spring sunshine lit her face. Yet deep inside she felt uneasy.

Can I run as well as I did when I had friends to cheer me on? she wondered. *I miss them. It's hard being the new kid in town.*

Looking around the field, she saw the long white lines someone had sprayed on the grass that morning. Everything was ready for the school field day. Yet Nat's thoughts weren't on the hundred-meter dash. Instead, she noticed Mona, a classmate who would be running against her.

I wish I could laugh and feel sure about myself the way she does, Nat thought.

Two months ago, after her family spent a lot of time praying about it, Nat's dad bought a restaurant in town. He believed God wanted them to be here. Nat had to admit she thought so, too. It wasn't always fun, working together in the restaurant, but she liked the Christian music Dad played for background.

Even so, it had been difficult changing schools in February. More than once Nat had wished her friends were here. *I want these kids to like me,* she thought. *Being alone makes it harder to be a Christian.*

Then she remembered one of the songs Dad played the night before. Trying to work up her courage, she hummed softly to herself.

"Good luck, Nat," said a voice behind her. "You'll do great!"

Nat turned, and gratitude welled up within her. It was just the encouragement she needed. "Thanks, Jared. Hope *you* do well!"

A moment later Jared was at the starting line, and Nat cheered from the sideline. Jared surged forward, settled into his stride, and crossed the finish line. A roar went up from the spectators.

Now it was Nat's turn. With all her heart she wanted to win. *Maybe then I'd feel part of this town,* she thought. Waiting at the starting line with Mona on her left, Nat prayed. *Help me, Lord. Help me.*

As she dug in for the start, she remembered the Scottish athlete Eric Liddell. By refusing to run on Sunday, he had sacrificed an Olympic gold medal. Yet he won the gold in a different event, then became a missionary to China.

Nat's prayer changed. *I want to honor you, Lord.*

"On your mark!" shouted the starter. "Set! Go!"

With a push Nat was off like a greyhound. Faster. Faster. Mona edged up. Out of the corner of her eye, Nat saw her and put on more speed. Feeling as if her lungs would burst, she crossed the finish line.

"Yaaaaaay, Nat!" came the cry. "Yaaaaaay, Nat!" But it was a halfhearted cheer.

Thank you, Jesus, she prayed as she walked back for her sweat shirt. *Thanks for helping me win.*

Her classmates gathered around her, offering congratulations. But Nat knew something was wrong. Soon most of them drifted over to where Mona stood.

As she watched them, Nat guessed their feelings. *It bothers them that I won. They've been together all their lives. They wanted Mona to get the best time.*

Ready to leave, Nat picked up her sweat shirt. The excitement she had felt in winning already sagged, like the air leaking out of a balloon.

As she turned away, Nat bumped into two kids standing behind her.

"New in town, aren't you?" asked the girl.

The boy next to her chimed in. "Your folks bought the restaurant, didn't they? You know, they really shouldn't play Christian music. Some people won't like it."

Nat's shoulders slumped. Her balloon of joy gave its final sputter of life. Where were Jared and the few others in this town who seemed to like her? With her whole heart, Nat wanted these kids to respect her, too.

Then another thought flashed through her mind. *Is this the real answer to my prayer? Where will I honor Jesus more—in winning the race or in what I say to these kids?*

Nat straightened, knowing she had to make a choice. For a moment she thought about it, wondering if the kids would laugh at her. Then she spoke. "Lots of people *do* like Christian music."

Deep inside, Nat knew she had won an even bigger race.

TO **TALK** ABOUT

▸ Nat could have answered, "Oh, that's just my parents' choice of music. I don't have anything to do with it." What cost was there for Nat to answer the way she did? How did she feel inside?

▸ Why did being new in town make it especially hard for Nat to stand up for her faith in Jesus?

▸ How does our wish to be liked get in the way of giving an answer that honors Jesus?

▸ **God doesn't expect us to always win, but He does ask us to always be faithful to Him.** What does it mean to be faithful?

▸ How can the Holy Spirit help us be faithful? Can you think of a time when He helped you to honor Jesus?

I have fought the good fight, I have finished the race, I have kept the faith. 2 Timothy 4:7

Jesus, it's hard to stand alone. With all my heart, I choose to be faithful to you. Give me the power of your Holy Spirit and the courage I need. Thank you that when kids make me feel lonely, you are still my best friend. Thank you that no matter what happens in my life, you will always be with me.

A Final Promise

Well, how are you doing? Have you been making some real-life choices? Have you discovered the secrets you unlock with every good choice? If so, you might like to know something more.

When you make the choice you believe Jesus wants, you may struggle afterward. You might ask yourself, *Did I do the right thing?* Or, if kids give you a hard time, you could think, *Well, I made the best choice. But I'm not worth anything. Nobody cares about me.* You feel miserable because you keep telling yourself you're worthless. Your feelings about yourself depend on whether others approve of you.

It's important to have approval from wise people who love God—your parents, teachers, pastor. It's not worth having approval from people who would force you to make wrong choices. Or from people who would make you feel sorry about good choices.

If you keep knocking yourself down, that can be harder to deal with than what other people think and say. God does just the opposite. When you make the choice you believe Jesus wants, the Holy Spirit will support you—if you let Him. He works in your good choices to help them become good habits. God also has special ways of showing that you are of value to Him.

Sometimes you know that right away because you sense His love for you. Other times it takes a while. It may even be hard to see. **When God honors you for being faithful to Him, it might not come in the way you think.** It may not come at the time you want. But it *will* come in God's best way!

The Bible gives God's word for it—a promise that encouraged Olympic hero Eric Liddell. You, too, can claim that promise at a moment of choice. "Those who honor me I will honor" (1 Samuel 2:30).

As you hang on tight to Jesus, may that secret also be yours.

Acknowledgments

Special thanks to all
who helped me make good choices
in writing this book:

The friends who faithfully prayed for me
My husband, Roy
Our son, Kevin, and his wife, Lyn
Chuck Peterson
Hope Erickson
Lois Carlson and Laurie Merritt
Charette Barta and Traci Mullins
Rochelle Glöege, Natasha Sperling,
Jack Major,
and the entire Bethany team

COME ABOARD!

With the Award-winning Author of **ADVENTURES OF THE NORTHWOODS**

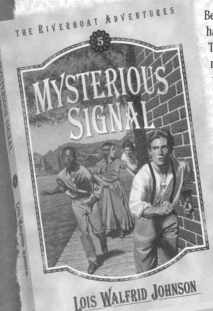

THE RIVERBOAT ADVENTURES

5

MYSTERIOUS SIGNAL

LOIS WALFRID JOHNSON

Bestselling author Lois Walfrid Johnson has more excitement in store for you with THE RIVERBOAT ADVENTURES. These carefully researched, historically accurate stories both thrill and educate boys and girls ages eight to thirteen. THE RIVERBOAT ADVENTURES dramatize the trials and blessings of working with the Underground Railroad and have met with enthusiastic support from parents, teachers, and young readers alike.

"...history is deftly woven into a fast-paced plot...an exciting read, with a thoughtful exploration of the slavery issue..." —Booklist

"Thank you very much for your great books: THE RIVERBOAT ADVENTURES. They are the best books I have ever read." —Bethany T.

THE RIVERBOAT ADVENTURES

1 Escape Into the Night
2 Race for Freedom
3 Midnight Rescue
4 The Swindler's Treasure
5 Mysterious Signal
6 The Fiddler's Secret

ADVENTURES OF THE NORTHWOODS

1 The Disappearing Stranger
2 The Hidden Message
3 The Creeping Shadows
4 The Vanishing Footprints
5 Trouble at Wild River
6 The Mysterious Hideaway

7 Grandpa's Stolen Treasure
8 The Runaway Clown
9 Mystery of the Missing
   Map
10 Disaster on Windy Hill

Available from your nearest Christian bookstore (800) 991-7747 or from Bethany House Publishers.

The Leader in Christian Fiction!
BETHANY HOUSE PUBLISHERS

11400 Hampshire Ave. South
Minneapolis, MN 55438

www.bethanyhouse.com